PURSUE YOUR SPARK

YOUR GUIDE TO ESCAPING MIDLIFE TRAPS, RECLAIMING CONFIDENCE, AND LIVING FULLY

HEIKE YATES

Pursue Your Spark

HEY Media
www.heikeyates.com

Cover design by Jeanly Zamora
Extracted by Cat Lopez
Edited by The Reaching & Rooted Publishing Team

ISBN: 978-1-961826-10-6 (Print)
ISBN: 978-1-961826-11-3 (ebook)

The information in this book is provided for informational purposes only. While the author and publisher have made every effort to ensure the accuracy and completeness of the information contained in this book, they assume no responsibility for errors, inaccuracies, omissions, or any inconsistency herein. Any slights of people, places, or organizations are unintentional.

Printed in United States

First Edition: August 2025

DEDICATION

To the midlife women ready to break free from the
ordinary and live a life that truly reflects who they are.
Your spark is your superpower—let it shine.

CONTENTS

FOREWORD

by Amy Thurman

There's a moment in every woman's life when she looks around and wonders, *How did I get here?* Not because she's ungrateful. Not because her life lacks meaning. But because somewhere along the way, between the roles she's played, the expectations she's carried, and the silence she's made peace with, it became harder to recognize the woman in the mirror.

If you're holding this book, I want you to know something:

You are not broken. You are not behind. And you are definitely not alone.

What Heike offers in these pages is more than a roadmap back to yourself; it's a permission slip to reclaim your spark without guilt, without shame, and without having to figure it all out overnight. The SPARK Framework she shares is simple, practical, and powerful; however, what truly makes this book shine is how she delivers it.

Heike's writing is refreshingly easy to read and understand, like talking to a wise, trusted friend who just *gets it*. Her voice is warm, direct, and relatable. And the real-life stories of Emma, Lisa, and Jasmine sprinkled throughout aren't just inspiring, they ground the journey in truth. You see yourself in these women. You feel their fears, their victories, and their progress. And something inside you starts to believe: *Maybe this is possible for me, too.*

PURSUE YOUR SPARK

This isn't a book that asks you to become someone new. It's a gentle, yet powerful guide that walks you back to who you've always been underneath the burnout, the busy, and the belief that you had to do it all alone.

You're not here to merely get by.

You're here to thrive.

So take a breath, turn the page, and let this be the moment you stop shrinking and start remembering who you are.

Let's begin.

—with spark and soul,

Amy Thurman
International Speaker, Best-Selling Author of Finding My Hero Within, and Polish the Mirror, Holding Space with Authentically Amy Podcast Host, Educator, Soul-Love Guru

WHY MIDLIFE MATTERS

WHAT IF MIDLIFE COULD BE THE MOST POWERFUL CHAPTER OF YOUR LIFE?

Before we dive in, pause for a moment.

When was the last time you felt *genuinely* curious about what you're capable of?

I'm not talking about the kind of curiosity that stops at *"What if?"* and leaves you stuck in overthinking. I'm talking about the type of curiosity that sparks action, the kind that pushes you beyond your comfort zone and asks:

"   *"What if I truly tried something different?"*   **"**

That's the curiosity I want you to bring to this book and your health and wellness journey. Because midlife isn't the end of your story. It's your time to get stronger, bolder, and be more in control than ever before.

I wrote this book for you—the midlife woman who feels something's missing.

You wake up tired, even after a full night's sleep. You stare at your workout clothes but decide maybe tomorrow. You reach for coffee because it's the only thing keeping you going. Deep down, you wonder—*is this just how life*

1

is now? Or does feeling strong and energized belong to a younger version of you? Or... could there be more waiting for you than you've let yourself imagine?

It's easy to believe that midlife is a slow decline, that feeling drained or frustrated is just part of the deal. But you don't have to stay stuck. You don't have to settle. Midlife isn't a time to fade into the background, it's your chance to step forward and take back your energy, confidence, and strength.

You have the power to make real, lasting changes that transform how you feel in your body and your life. And this book will show you how.

I KNOW WHAT IT FEELS LIKE TO BE STUCK.

There was a moment I'll never forget. I was rushing out the door, juggling errands, mom duties, and everything else on my plate when I caught my reflection in a store window. My shoulders were slumped. My eyes looked tired. And the spark I once had? Gone. I barely recognized the woman staring back at me.

That moment stopped me in my tracks. I thought, *"Is this just how it is now? Is this who I am?"*

I had poured so much of myself into caring for everyone else—my kids, my responsibilities, my new life in a new country—that somewhere along the way, I lost sight of *me*. I wasn't even on my own list anymore. I was running on autopilot, showing up for everyone but myself, hoping that somehow things would just get better.

That was my breaking point.

But instead of chasing another quick-fix diet or dragging myself through punishing workouts hoping for change, I made a different choice.

I gave myself permission to start small, and to start exactly where I was.

I focused on moving in a way that felt good. I let go of the pressure to be perfect and just showed up. I gave myself grace when I needed rest and celebrated the days I showed up with strength. I stopped trying to force my way "back" and instead created a path forward to fit *me*.

And slowly, everything began to shift. My energy came back. My confidence returned. Most importantly, I felt like *me* again—strong, vibrant, and fully alive.

That experience didn't just change how I moved through my days. It became the foundation for everything I teach now.

So if you're feeling stuck, tired, or disconnected from yourself, I want you to know that I see you. And I wrote this book for you.

HOW I TURNED IT AROUND—AND HOW YOU CAN, TOO

I didn't have a master plan. I didn't even know where to begin. But I knew I couldn't keep waiting to feel ready. So I started small. With no real background in fitness, I signed up for classes at the local YMCA in Maryland. I showed up feeling unsure, even a little out of place, but I kept going. I followed along, mimicked the movements, watched the instructors closely, and tried to understand what worked. With each class, I felt a little stronger. I learned how to move, how to challenge myself, and how to build a routine. Eventually, I began practicing at home, tiny steps that added up. What I didn't know then was that I was laying the foundation for what would one day become my career. And it's the same kind of foundation *you* can start building—one simple action at a time.

Instead of forcing myself into programs designed for twenty-somethings, I focused on movement that felt good, not exhausting. I chose strength over punishment. And I let go of the pressure to get back to my "old self" and started building a version of me that felt stronger than ever before.

As I rebuilt my confidence, I realized something powerful: I wasn't alone in this struggle.

The more I talked to other women, the more I heard the same frustration. They felt exhausted, stuck, and unsure how to create lasting change. They were caught in the same cycles I had been, the all-or-nothing mindset, where they either went all in or gave up entirely.

Overwhelmed by everything they thought they *had* to change, many of them secretly wondered, *why even bother?* And then there was the comparison; they were always measuring themselves against who they were in their thirties, feeling like they should be further along by now.

They didn't realize they were stuck in patterns, traps really, that were holding them back. That's when I knew I had to step in and help women break free—not by doing more, but by doing it differently.

I became a certified fitness and nutrition coach, and over the past four decades, I've helped thousands of midlife women reclaim their energy, rebuild their strength, and finally feel like themselves again.

What came out of that journey is now the Five-Step SPARK Framework: a simple, doable system that will help you break free from what's holding you back and build a strong, confident, energized midlife.

Being healthy and strong doesn't have to be complicated. It starts with small, consistent actions—so simple you might not even notice the impact at first. But trust me, those actions stack up. And before you know it, you're living the change you once thought was out of reach.

Let's take that first step together.

YOU GOT THIS. IT'S TIME TO PURSUE YOUR SPARK!

Midlife Time Management Planner   Workout Progressions

Accountability Tracker   Meal Prep Cheatsheet

How To Measure Portions   3 Day Meal Ideas

(Are you a notetaker? Scan the QR code above to access supplemental worksheets, materials, and journal prompts to support you along the way.)

INTRODUCTION

The other day, my client Tamara walked into my studio, all smiles and beaming. She had been away for a few days visiting her daughter Nancy in Baltimore, MD, without her husband. They spent their time hanging out together, exploring the city, drinking coffee at one of the little street cafés, and having long mother-daughter talks. They had no care in the world or time constraints to be somewhere at a specific time. She looked at me, eyes shining, and said, "Heike, I felt like myself again!"

I've worked with Tamara for years. Every week, she steps away from the demands of her life for one uninterrupted hour of Pilates. Over time, I've come to know her beyond just fitness, her struggles, resilience, and the burdens she carries.

Tamara had always been strong and active. But over the years, her body began to change in ways she didn't expect. After facing a series of serious health challenges, she told me it felt like her body had betrayed her. The confidence she once carried so easily started to fade. Movement, which had always been her outlet, became something she struggled with, physically and emotionally. But we didn't give up. We adjusted. We found new ways for her to move, to feel capable, and to stay connected to her strength. Little by little, she started to trust her body again and herself.

Then, her husband's health began to decline. Suddenly, her struggles took a backseat. Doctor's appointments filled her calendar. Grocery shopping, cooking, managing the house, everything revolved around his needs. His world became her world. She stopped meeting friends for walks, skipped her singing group, and hesitated before making plans, constantly asking herself, *What if he needs me?*

She felt tethered to the house and his needs. The one hour of Pilates per week felt like she was sneaking away to have time for herself. She felt guilty when she wanted to meet up with her friends for a walk or go to the gym or her beloved singing group.

Tamara started to wonder if this was just how life would be from now on. Was this it? Was midlife just exhaustion, duty, and always putting yourself last?

Then, she took that trip.

For the first time in years, she stepped away from the weight of responsibility. She walked through bustling streets with nothing but time, let conversations with her daughter linger without checking the clock, and felt the sun's warmth on her face as she sat at a café, simply being.

And in that space, something shifted.

She felt free. Light. Present. Like she was stepping back into herself after years of feeling lost in the daily grind.

That day, standing in my studio, I knew something had changed. She wasn't just relieved from her responsibilities for a weekend, she had reconnected with a part of herself she hadn't realized was missing.

FEELING DISCONNECTED

Have you ever had one of those moments where you suddenly realize you don't feel like yourself anymore? Maybe it's just a passing thought; something feels *off*, but you brush it aside, hoping it's just a phase. Other times, that feeling lingers. Days turn into weeks, then months, until one day, you look in the mirror and barely recognize the person staring back at you.

It's like a slow drift. You can't quite pinpoint when it started or why, but you just know you're not as excited or energized as you once were. You want something to change, but where do you even begin?

That sense of disconnect isn't just in your head. It's real. It's that nagging feeling that there's a gap between who you are now and who you could be.

What causes that disconnect in the first place?

Let's take a closer look.

HERE IS WHY THIS HAPPENS

So, what causes this sense of disconnect—or that *gap*—between where you are now and where you want to be? It's not that you're doing anything wrong. It's that life shifted, your body, your priorities, your energy and no one showed you how to adapt. That gap isn't failure. It's a signal. And once you understand what's behind it, you can stop second-guessing yourself and start building the life you actually want to live.

Often, it's a combination of physical changes, stress, life transitions, and information overload. Here are a few key factors, along with short stories to illustrate how they might unfold in real life:

HORMONAL SHIFTS

Midlife hormone changes can throw everything off, from mood, stress, appetite, and even body image. My friend Dana felt off for weeks, stuck in a fog of anxiety and exhaustion. She couldn't figure out why she felt that way, until she realized her hormones were out of balance. Once she knew what was happening, she worked with her doctor to adjust her routine, and little by little, she started feeling like herself again.

CHRONIC STRESS AND OVERWHELM

I've been there: working full-time at a health club, raising two kids alone, and traveling on weekends to teach fitness classes. I thought I could "power through," but the exhaustion caught up with me. One day, I saw my reflection in the gym mirror and barely recognized myself. I was running on fumes, completely drained.

That moment was a wake-up call. I realized I had been giving everything to everyone else, my clients, my kids, my job, while putting myself dead last. I kept pushing through, convinced that rest was a luxury I couldn't afford. But the truth was, ignoring my needs wasn't just exhausting; it was unsustainable.

LIFE TRANSITIONS

Retirement, an empty nest, a career change, or divorce can all leave you wondering: *What's next?* One client told me, "Ever since my youngest left for college, I don't know what to do with myself. My days used to be so full. Now, I feel like I have no purpose."

CONFLICTING INFORMATION

It's impossible to scroll through the internet without being hit with the latest "must-try" health trend. One day, it's all about Keto. Next, it's Paleo. Then, suddenly, carbs aren't the enemy anymore, but now you should be cutting out dairy, or maybe it's seed oils?

My client Jane got caught in this exact cycle. Every time she read about a new "miracle" diet, she jumped in, hoping *this one* would finally be the answer. She bounced from one trend to the next, Keto, Paleo, plant-based, Whole30, trying so hard to "do it right" that, before she knew it, she had no idea what 'right' even meant anymore.

One day, she looked at me, frustration written all over her face. *"Should I be eating carbs? Avoiding them? Is dairy good or bad? What about protein?"* Her voice was filled with exhaustion, like she was carrying the weight of every conflicting diet rule she had ever read.

She had tried so hard to get it *right* that she had completely lost trust in herself. Instead of listening to her body, she was stuck in a loop of second-guessing every bite. She wasn't just overwhelmed, she felt powerless.

FEAR AND INACTION

Sometimes it shows up as a tight knot in your chest when you think about making a change. Other times, it's just a vague sense of restlessness or frustration you can't quite explain. You might feel exhausted and know, deep down, that something needs to shift, but the idea of *where to even begin* feels overwhelming. Or maybe you haven't even gotten that far, just moving through your days on autopilot, wondering if this is all there is.

Maybe you've tried before, only to fall back into the same patterns. Or maybe you keep telling yourself, "I'll start next week." But somehow, next week always gets pushed further away. Instead of taking small steps, you wait for the "perfect" time, the "right" plan, the guarantee that you won't fail this time.

But that moment never comes.

So you stay in place knowing you need a change, but paralyzed by the fear of getting it wrong. And the longer you wait, the harder it feels to begin.

It's frustrating, because deep down, you don't just *want* things to be different. You *need* them to be.

So why is it so hard to take the first step?

KEEP MOVING FORWARD, ONE STEP AT A TIME, AND WATCH HOW YOUR LIFE STARTS TO SPARK!

UNDERSTANDING THE DISCONNECT

The longer we feel out of sync with our goals and desires, the harder it becomes to believe we can change. We start questioning ourselves: *Why can't I stick with anything? What's wrong with me? Maybe you've even forgotten what feeling like yourself actually feels like.*

Over time, doubt creeps in. We tell ourselves we need the *perfect* plan before starting and that if we can't do everything right from day one, maybe it's not worth trying. And so, we wait. We scroll past fitness routines, meal plans, and success stories on social media, feeling like everyone else has it figured out. Meanwhile, we're stuck watching, wishing, but not moving.

And that's how we get caught in a cycle of inaction.

Change starts to feel impossible because the habits that hold us back often fly under the radar. But here's the thing: those doubts, excuses, invisible barriers are not the truth. They're just stories we've told ourselves for so long that we've started to believe them.

At the core of it all is that same disconnect you've been feeling, the space between where you are now and where you want to be. It hides beneath the frustration, the fatigue, the sense that something just isn't working.

The good news? You can finally move forward once you recognize what's holding you back.

And that's precisely what we're going to do next.

Let's take a closer look at the hidden ways these barriers show up in your life so you can finally break free and start feeling like yourself again.

CHAPTER 1

INVISIBLE BARRIERS HOLDING YOU BACK

For so many midlife women, prioritizing themselves feels impossible. It's not that they don't want to make a change; it's that life constantly gets in the way. Time constraints, fear, and a lack of boundaries gradually steal their attention, making it feel like there's never a right moment to focus on themselves.

But here's the thing. Most barriers holding us back are not physical. They are invisible.

We tell ourselves we don't have time, we are too busy caring for everyone else, and now is not the right time to start. We convince ourselves we need to have all the answers before we begin.

These beliefs keep us stuck. And I know this feeling well because I have been there.

After leaving my career in foreign service and moving to Bethesda, Maryland, everything changed. I was home with a baby, exhausted, out of shape, and completely untethered. I didn't recognize my body anymore. I had gained fifty pounds during my pregnancy, and every attempt to get "back in shape" just left me more frustrated, more defeated. I wasn't just tired—I was *lost*. I didn't know who I was without my career. I didn't feel confident in my body. I kept thinking, *I don't know what to do. I don't have the answers. Maybe this is just how it is now.* That was the hardest part, the fear that maybe the gap between the life I had and the life I wanted was permanent.

Then, a friend invited me to an exercise class at the local YMCA. I had never done anything like it before, but I showed up. The class was in a small basement gym, led by a woman in spandex with a boombox. I followed along, clumsy and uncertain, but something clicked. I wasn't just working out, I was moving. And it felt good.

I kept going back, even when my son cried in the daycare the entire time. It was the one thing that was just for me and nothing was going to stop me.

One day, the instructor asked if I had ever considered becoming a fitness teacher. I laughed. Me? Teach a class? That invisible barrier showed up again, the voice telling me I wasn't qualified, that I wasn't fit enough, that I didn't belong. And there was another fear lingering beneath it, one I wasn't quite ready to face.

But this time, I didn't listen.

I took the leap, even though I had no idea what I was doing. My first tryout was a disaster. I couldn't follow the beat of the music, and the coach told me I wasn't ready. I was devastated. But I practiced relentlessly, came back four weeks later, and passed the test.

That moment shattered the belief that I had to have everything figured out before I could begin.

From there, my fitness journey took off. I became a group fitness instructor, teaching everything from step aerobics to prenatal classes. I fell in love with movement, got my American Council of Exercise Personal Trainer Certification, and eventually managed the aerobics program at a health club. I started collecting certifications like candy, at one point, I had up to fifteen.

Over time, I continued to grow, earning certifications in Pilates, strength training, functional movement, osteoporosis exercises, and sports nutrition.

And it all started with one small decision.

Some of those early certifications aren't active anymore, but they still hold a special place in my heart, step aerobics, kickboxing, water aerobics, slide, even spinning. It was a wild, wonderful ride.

Each of these represented a step forward, not just in my career but in proving to myself that I could do this. But my journey wasn't a straight path. Like so many women, I had responsibilities pulling me in different directions with kids to care for, a divorce to navigate, and the constant struggle of balancing my ambitions with reality.

There were so many invisible barriers along the way, time constraints, fear of failing, and the constant pressure to do it all without missing a beat. Some days, it felt like I was barely keeping my head above water. But I kept going. Not because I had it all figured out, but because something inside me refused to give up. I learned by doing. I stumbled, got back up, and slowly started piecing together a version of life that felt more like *me*. I took on challenges I never thought I was capable of. I pushed past comfort zones. And little by little, I began bridging the gap between where I was and who I was becoming.

NOTHING CAN STOP ME NOW!

At 36, I stepped on stage as a bodybuilder, starting to believe that strength is ageless. By 38, I found myself diving into yoga, not because I had some grand plan but out of pure necessity.

The health club where I worked had only one yoga instructor, and members kept asking for more classes. I thought, *What if she quits? What if something happens?* So, I decided to study with her and take her classes, just in case. She taught B.K.S. Iyengar Yoga—a style focused on alignment and precision— and I soaked it up. I figured, if nothing else, I'd be prepared if the club ever needed a backup instructor.

And wouldn't you know it? One day, she left with no warning or backup plan. Just gone. And suddenly, I was standing in front of an entire class. The problem? I wasn't certified.

I grabbed my notepad, looked at the class, and told them straight up: *I'm not certified, but I've been practicing for years and can lead you through a solid class.* And they believed in me. More than that, they *trusted* me.

But I didn't stop there. While everyone else was teaching Pilates the traditional way, I saw an opportunity to do something new. At 39, I developed the first-ever program combining the Pilates matwork with the stability ball, something no one had done before. That idea became Pilates with Resist-A-Ball, a teacher training program that spread far beyond what I ever imagined.

There were so many moments where it would've been easier to quit, when I wasn't certified, when I doubted myself, when I decided to step outside the norm and create something new. But I kept going. I chose belief over fear.

And I see this all the time with the women I coach. Things don't go as expected, support falls through, and before they know it, they're stuck, questioning themselves and wondering if real change is even possible.

But here's the thing: You don't have to stay stuck.

You might not be navigating a yoga class or a Pilates certification, but maybe you've had moments when the plan completely fell apart.

Maybe you started a fitness routine but got injured. Maybe you tried to change your diet but felt overwhelmed by all the conflicting advice. Maybe you're so busy caring for everyone else that you no longer know what you want

These are your invisible barriers, the ones that whisper: *Maybe now isn't the right time. Maybe I should wait until things settle down. Maybe I'm just not cut out for this.*

BUT WHAT IF YOU DIDN'T WAIT?

What if that obstacle wasn't a sign to stop, but a gentle nudge to take a different path, one that leads somewhere even better?

That's exactly what we're going to explore next.

Breaking down barriers is just the first step. The real question is, what happens next?

When the excuses fade, when the roadblocks start to crumble, when you finally allow yourself to consider something *more*, what do you do with that space?

This is where curiosity steps in.

CHAPTER 2

A JOURNEY FUELED BY CURIOSITY

B reaking invisible barriers is the first step. To gain the confidence needed to do it, we have to believe there is something more on the other side. But how do you get there when doubt, hesitation, and past failures keep pulling you back?

It starts with curiosity.

Not the passive kind of curiosity that wonders, "What if?" And stops there. I'm talking about the type of curiosity that sparks action. The kind that makes you lean in instead of pulling away. The kind that asks, "What if I did try something different? What if I stopped waiting for the perfect time? What if I took one small step to see what would happen?"

That's the curiosity I want you to bring to this book and your health and wellness journey. Curiosity isn't only about asking questions. It's about daring to explore the answers.

So, as you move forward, get curious about yourself. What excites you? What challenges you? What's one thing you've been telling yourself isn't possible?

And most importantly, what if it is possible?

HOW ONE RACE CHANGED EVERYTHING

It's 2008, and I'm standing at the starting line of the Cherry Blossom 10-Miler, in Washington, D.C., feeling the electric energy of the crowd. The funny thing? I hadn't even planned on running this race.

One of my clients had a last-minute conflict and gave me her race entry. I figured, "Why not?" I hadn't trained specifically for it, I was only running about three miles at the time, and this would be the longest distance I'd ever run. But I was curious. I wanted to see what I was capable of.

So, I ran it.

And I loved it.

That single race sparked something in me, an excitement, a hunger for a bigger challenge. Instead of just moving on, I leaned into that curiosity. Later that year, I signed up for the Montgomery County Road Runners beginner marathon program. I thought, *This is fun, why not take the next big step and run a marathon?* The truth? I had no idea what I was getting myself into.

At one of my first training runs, I asked my coach, "What should my goal be for this marathon?"

His response? "Well, you're a first-timer. You should just focus on finishing."

That answer didn't sit well with me.

I didn't just want to finish, I wanted to see what I was capable of. During training, the head coach Andy pulled me aside and said, "If you finish this race, you could qualify to run the Boston Marathon next year." That simple statement changed everything. Suddenly, the goal wasn't just to get across the finish line, it was to chase something I never thought possible. A Boston qualifying time meant finishing in four hours. It felt bold, maybe even impossible. But it lit a spark. And that was all I needed.

Fast forward to race day: the Marine Corps Marathon in Washington, D.C., my very first marathon. I had trained hard, but I wasn't doing it alone. My friend Patricia and I had planned to run the entire race together, side by side, just like we trained. And for most of the race, we did. But around mile 22, things changed. Patricia started to slow down, she hadn't taken in enough nutrition during the race, and I could see it in her eyes. She looked at me and said, "Go get Boston, Heike."

I hesitated for a second. Leaving her felt hard. But those words lit a fire in me. I picked up my pace, legs burning, heart pounding, not just to finish, but to chase something bigger. When I crossed the finish line, I couldn't believe it: 3 hours and 50 minutes. I had qualified for the Boston Marathon, with ten minutes to spare. I was in shock, exhausted… and completely exhilarated. I had done something I once thought was impossible.

None of that would have happened if I had let my doubts, limitations, or fear of the unknown stop me. It all started with one question:

" *What if I went for it?* **"**

That's the power of curiosity. You don't have to know exactly where it will take you, you just have to be willing to begin.

CURIOSITY IS YOUR GREATEST ADVANTAGE

Think about the times you've wanted to change but felt stuck. Maybe the thought of starting a new fitness routine or overhauling your nutrition felt hard.

Now, what if you looked at it differently? What if change didn't have to be overwhelming? What if you approached it with curiosity?

That's exactly what Patty did.

She showed up at my studio for her first session and stood right inside the doorway, like she wasn't sure if she wanted to step in. She clutched her water bottle, shifting it from one hand to the other.

"This feels... weird," she admitted, giving a small, nervous laugh. "I don't know what I'm doing."

Patty had never been to a private studio, taken a class, or worked with a trainer. The thought of starting from square one after all these years felt intimidating.

"What if I can't do this?" she blurted out. "What if I don't have the coordination or the strength?"

I smiled and gestured toward the mat. "Well...what if you just try?" She exhaled, hesitated for a second, then finally nodded. "Okay. Just try."

And so, she did.

She followed my lead, moving cautiously at first, feeling out each new exercise. Instead of worrying about whether she was doing it *right*, she focused on how it felt. Instead of stressing about keeping up, she let herself be curious about what she could do.

Session by session, something shifted.

One day, as she finished a set of lunges, she straightened up, wiped her forehead, and grinned. "I think I actually like this." She laughed as if the thought had never occurred to her.

Curiosity had turned what once felt intimidating into something doable. It allowed her to explore, experiment, and see what her body could do without the pressure of perfection. And one day, without even realizing it, she stopped "trying" and started doing.

Curiosity made that possible.

CURIOSITY OVERCOMES FEAR AND DOUBT

I used to think I just needed more discipline. But the truth? Fear of failure and self-doubt were what really kept me stuck. I've hesitated, overthought, and talked myself out of things before I even began. I was so worried I wouldn't follow through that I froze up entirely.

But I've learned that curiosity is the antidote to fear. Fear whispers, "What if I fail?" Curiosity asks, "What if I learn something new?" Fear says, "I'm not good enough." Curiosity wonders, "What if I just tried?"

Take a moment when you've felt disappointed in yourself. Maybe you tried a new workout and struggled to keep up, or you started a new habit and didn't stick with it as long as you hoped. It's easy to get discouraged, to take that as proof that you're not good enough or that change isn't possible.

But what if you got curious instead? What did I learn about my body today? What slight shift could help me next time? How can I make this work in a way that feels good?

Curiosity takes the pressure off. It reframes failure as feedback. It shifts your mindset from self-doubt to possibility. That's where real progress happens.

Violet, one of my clients, spent years stuck in the loop of "What if I can't?" She wanted to feel strong again—to move with confidence, to trust her body—but every time she thought about starting something new, self-doubt shut it down. Then one day, after trying on a pair of pants that no longer fit and feeling completely defeated, she asked herself a new question: "What if I just tried?"

She signed up for a beginner Pilates class, nervous, unsure, almost canceling at the last minute. But she showed up. That first class wasn't perfect. She wobbled, got confused, and felt out of place. But she also laughed, felt her muscles fire, and remembered what it felt like to try.

That's when everything started to shift. Violet realized she didn't need to be more flexible, more fit, or more ready. She just needed to begin.

The best part? You don't need all the answers right now. This isn't about perfection. It's about being willing to take that first step with curiosity leading the way.

CURIOSITY KEEPS YOU MOVING FORWARD

Starting is one thing. Staying engaged and motivated? That's where curiosity shines.

Routines can get stale. Motivation fades. The same workouts, meals, and habits that once felt exciting can start to feel... meh. And that's exactly when most people give up, not because they failed, but because they got bored.

Curiosity keeps things fresh, turns plateaus into experiments, and shifts the focus from doing things perfectly to exploring new possibilities.

Instead of getting frustrated when progress slows, curiosity helps you ask better questions: What if I tried a new challenge, something totally different? How can I make this more fun? What small tweak could bring my energy back?

It may mean adding strength training or Pilates. Maybe it's dancing, hiking, or even paddleboarding. Movement doesn't have to look one way to be effective, it just has to spark something in you.

The same goes for food. If your meals feel like a boring loop of grilled chicken and steamed veggies, shake things up. Try a new spice blend, roast a different seasonal veggie, or prep a batch of protein you actually *want* to eat.

Curiosity leads to creativity and that's how healthy eating becomes something you enjoy, not just endure.

The key isn't just sticking to a plan, it's staying engaged in the process. Because when you're curious, you're more willing to try, adjust, and keep going. That's what creates lasting results.

CURIOSITY: THE KEY TO CHANGE

Curiosity makes change possible, even when you don't feel ready. It helps you move from hesitation to action, from self-doubt to possibility.

The challenge is that many of us get stuck at "what if?" We wonder what it would be like to feel stronger, more energized, more confident. But instead of exploring, we freeze, afraid of failing again or doing it wrong.

Curiosity changes that. It asks, "What if I tried?" and lets that be enough to begin, not with a perfect plan but with a willingness to see what happens.

Imagine approaching your health like a curious experiment instead of a rigid program. There's no need to get everything right, you're just collecting data. Start by asking: *What movement feels doable today? What meals leave me feeling energized instead of sluggish? What routines actually fit my real life?*

Curiosity turns trial and error into progress.

This mindset removes the pressure to have everything figured out. It creates space for trial and error, for learning, and for growth.

And while curiosity gets you started and helps you stay engaged, it's not always enough. Because as soon as you try something new, you'll meet resistance, roadblocks, doubt, frustration. That's when you'll need something else: self-compassion. The grace to keep going even when it's messy. The kindness of treating yourself like someone worth showing up for.

CURIOSITY OPENS THE DOOR. SELF-COMPASSION HELPS YOU WALK THROUGH IT.

SELF-COMPASSION: THE MISSING PIECE

If curiosity is what gets you started, self-compassion is what keeps you going.

Most people believe that being hard on themselves will make them more disciplined. But research (and experience) shows the opposite is true: shame and self-criticism don't motivate us. They paralyze us.

It starts with the best intentions. You decide to commit to a new routine, and then life happens. You miss a workout or eat something that wasn't part of the plan. Instead of adjusting, the negative thoughts creep in: *I messed up. I'll never get this right. I always quit anyway.*

Discouraged and ashamed, you stop trying altogether. That all-or-nothing mindset, the belief that if you can't do it perfectly, it's not worth doing at all, is what keeps so many women stuck in a cycle of starting and stopping.

But what if, instead of beating yourself up, you offered yourself compassion?

> " *What if you reminded yourself, "I had a rough day, but that doesn't mean I failed."*
> *What if you said, "One missed workout doesn't erase all the progress I've made."*
> *What if you believed, "It's okay not to be perfect. What matters is that I keep going."* "

Self-compassion removes the guilt and shame that make us want to give up. It shifts the story from "I messed up" to "I'm learning, and I'm still in this." Because real change isn't about being flawless, it's about staying in the game, even when it's messy.

Imagine how much further you'd go if, instead of quitting every time you stumbled, you gave yourself permission to adjust and keep moving forward with kindness and grace.

FACING YOUR DEEPEST FEARS

Curiosity and self-compassion are powerful, but they're not always enough. Because beneath the surface, there's often something deeper holding us back.

YOUR DEEPEST FEARS SAYS...

> *What if I try and still fail?*
> *What if I never get back to where I used to be?*
> *What if I look foolish?*
> *What if people judge me?*
> *What if I have to admit I don't know what I'm doing?*

These aren't just passing thoughts. They shape how we show up, or don't. They keep us playing small, building invisible walls between where we are and where we want to be.

And when those fears go unchecked, they start to feel like truth.

That's when something else begins to grow: a gap.

That space between the life you're living and the one you want. It's not always obvious. Sometimes it just feels like a low hum of frustration, like something's missing, but you can't quite name what.

And when we don't recognize that gap for what it is, we fall into patterns. Traps. Beliefs and behaviors that keep us stuck, even when we desperately want to move forward.

But here's the good news:

Just because the gap is there doesn't mean you can't bridge it. Just because you've fallen into the trap before doesn't mean you have to stay there.

And that's exactly what we're going to explore next.

CHAPTER 3

WHAT IS THE GAP AND WHY ARE YOU STILL STUCK?

Alright, it's time to mind the gap and no, we're not talking about the space between the train and the platform. We're talking about the invisible space that keeps you from becoming the person you want to be.

The gap isn't just about goals. It's the invisible space between who you are now and the version of you that feels strong, healthy, and confident. Maybe you picture that version clearly, but instead of moving forward, you're stuck in a loop.

You may long to feel comfortable in your body again, but every time you try to make a change, self-doubt creeps in. Or you want to prioritize yourself more, yet life, responsibilities, and everyone else's needs always seem to come first. That space between your reality and your desires? That's the gap.

And here's the thing: gaps are normal. They exist in all areas of life: health, career, relationships, and personal growth.

Some gaps motivate us to take action. Others leave us feeling defeated, like we'll never close the distance.

WHY DO GAPS FEEL SO HARD TO CLOSE?

The problem isn't that the gap exists, it's what we do (or don't do) when we notice it. Some people look at the distance between where they are and where they want to be and feel overwhelmed, so they don't start at all.

Others ignore the gap. They convince themselves that where they are now is "good enough" even if, deep down, they want something more.

Some try to jump across the gap too fast, demanding instant results. When they don't see results overnight, they quit.

But here's what most people don't realize:

Gaps don't just sit there. If we ignore them, they grow. And over time, they turn into traps, patterns that keep us stuck in the same loop.

Maybe you've felt it before. You sense something's off. You want things to be different, so you try to make a change. But the old habits creep back in. Motivation fades. You start to wonder, "Maybe I'm just not cut out for this."

And just like that, the gap becomes a trap, a cycle of starting and stopping, trying and giving up, over and over again.

So the real question is: What kind of gap are you stuck in?

In the next few pages, we'll unpack the most common types of gaps that lead to hesitation, procrastination, or self-doubt, so that you can finally name what's been holding you back.

Because once you can name it, you can start to change it.

BUT THAT'S NOT ENOUGH

Naming the gap is a powerful first step, but awareness alone doesn't create change.

Because those gaps? They're not just emotional or mental. They're reinforced by patterns, traps you fall into again and again, even when you *know* better. Sometimes, it's not a lack of effort or knowledge that keeps you stuck. It's the invisible forces pulling you back into old habits, outdated beliefs, and second-guessing.

That's exactly what was happening with my client Dawn.

She sat across from me, arms crossed, frustration all over her face. "I don't get it," she sighed. "I know exactly what to do. I've read all the books, followed all the experts. Even my son says, 'Mom, you don't need a coach, you already know this stuff!'"

And yet... she was stuck.

Every Monday, she told herself she'd start. And every Monday came and went. She had good intentions. Solid routines. Smart strategies. But when it came time to actually do them, something always got in the way.

"I just can't seem to follow through," she admitted. "I don't understand why."

Dawn wasn't lazy. She wasn't unmotivated. She didn't need more information.

But the gap between what she *knew* and what she *did* kept getting wider. And the longer she stayed stuck, the more discouraged she felt.

Dawn's story isn't rare. So many women are living in that same tension, knowing what they want, knowing what to do, and still feeling stuck. That's why awareness alone isn't enough. We have to understand the *type* of gap we're in and the trap that's holding us there.

In the next section, we'll explore the five major gaps that keep so many women from moving forward, even when they know they're ready for something more.

WHAT ARE THE 5 MAJOR GAPS?

Let's get into some common gaps that many of us grapple with as we navigate our midlife journeys. Whether it's the sneaky Confidence Gap that whispers doubts into our ears, the Knowledge Gap that holds us back with its silent "you don't know enough yet," the Support Gap that can leave us feeling isolated, the Expectation Gap that traps us in outdated norms, or the Visibility Gap that can render us invisible in crowded spaces, each of these gaps plays a significant role in shaping our experiences.

THE CONFIDENCE GAP

It's a sneaky little one, whispering doubt into our ears when we're about to try something new or change our habits. *I'm not ready to join that fitness class. I can't switch up my diet.* It's not about confidence, it's about how doubt can shape our choices, often without us even realizing it.

Confidence impacts everything, from the exercises we dare to try to the food we believe is worth prioritizing. It shapes how we feel about ourselves and whether we believe we can actually stick with new habits. When confidence is low, it's easy to hold back from trying something new or pushing past old limits.

Take Violet, for example. She used to walk past the Pilates studio, convinced she wasn't flexible enough to join. She kept telling herself she would start once she felt "ready." She realized she'd been walking past that studio for over a year, stuck in the same story. That day, she thought, *"If not now, when?"* and signed up for a beginner class. She was nervous and unsure of herself, but by the end of the class, something shifted. She didn't need to be more flexible or more "ready." She just needed to show up. That's when she realized that she had been capable all along.

The confidence gap isn't just about our fitness choices. It shows up at the dinner table, in social settings, and in the way we talk to ourselves. It is the reason someone hesitates to cook a homemade meal because they think they'll mess it up. It's why we second-guess ourselves at the table, giving in to peer pressure instead of ordering what we *actually* want. Not because we don't know better, but because we don't feel confident enough to stand by our choices.

Building confidence is not about having everything figured out. It is about taking small, bold steps forward. The more we challenge self-doubt, the more we prove to ourselves that we are stronger, braver, and more capable than we thought.

THE KNOWLEDGE GAP

Now let's talk about the knowledge gap. This one's sneaky. It's that space between what we actually know... and what we *think* we know. And yep, that gap can mess with how we eat, move, and take care of ourselves.

There is no shortage of health advice out there. One expert tells you to eat more protein; another says plant-based is the way to go. One fitness plan preaches high-intensity workouts, and others swear by low-impact movement. With so much conflicting information, it is easy to feel overwhelmed and confused about what works.

You are not alone in this.

Closing the knowledge gap is a game-changer. It helps us stop guessing and start understanding what's really going on in our bodies. That's how we make choices that feel right, work long-term, and actually help us thrive.

For years, Melissa had been doing the same workout routine. Cardio, light weights, a little stretching, thinking it was enough to stay strong and fit. But no matter how hard she worked, she never saw the progress she expected. Frustrated, she assumed something was wrong with her body.

Then, she learned about progressive overload. This is a principle of gradually increasing resistance to build strength. She realized that instead of pushing herself harder, she needed to train smarter. A few simple adjustments, like increasing weights and varying her workouts, completely changed her results. The problem was not effort, it was a gap in knowledge.

Not knowing keeps us stuck. Whether it's around workouts, food, or how to even set a goal, that lack of clarity chips away at our confidence. But once we understand what works for *us*, making healthier choices starts to feel a lot easier.

Keep in mind that more information is not always the answer. Knowing something does not mean we will apply it. The real challenge is learning how to filter through the noise, trust ourselves, and put what we learn into action in a way that works for us.

THE SUPPORT GAP

Jumping into the support gap, this one is about the power of having cheerleaders in your corner. Whether it is a food accountability partner, someone who lifts your spirits, or a workout buddy you see a few times a week, support can be the difference between pushing forward and giving up. It is like having a safety net that catches you when you stumble and cheers you on when you succeed.

Building a trusting community keeps us motivated and moving forward with our fitness and nutrition goals. Because, let's face it, everything's a bit easier when you're not alone.

Your support network doesn't have to be a fitness coach or accountability buddy (though that helps!). It could be a lifelong friend, a coworker you still text, or even an online group that gets what you're going through. What matters most is surrounding yourself with people who lift you up, keep you on track, and remind you that you're in this *with* others.

Support provides emotional reinforcement and helps maintain a positive mindset. It makes all the difference. Having people in your corner increases motivation to stick to your goals, even if you don't realize it.

For years, Karen tried to stay consistent with exercise, but life always seemed to get in the way. She would start strong, and then lose motivation after a few weeks. One day, a friend invited her to join a small outdoor fitness group class. At first, she hesitated, unsure if she would fit in. But after one session, she realized something. She was not showing up for herself, she was showing up for the group.

Knowing the group was expecting her to show up made it easier to stay committed. On the days she felt like skipping, someone would text her, "See you tonight?" That little nudge made all the difference. And over time, those small moments of accountability turned into a habit that stuck and she loved going to her class.

Support isn't just about clapping from the sidelines. It's about having people who check in, lift you up, and remind you that your goals matter. That kind of support can turn "I'm on my own" into "I've got this—because I've got people that support me. .

THE EXPECTATION GAP

Ready to ditch the "shoulds" and "supposed tos" that society keeps throwing at us? That's the expectation gap. It's where we stop living by someone else's rules and start owning what *really* matters to us.

It's not about checking boxes or chasing someone else's version of success. It's about creating a path that reflects *your* values, *your* health, and what makes *you* feel good. That's when things start to shift, when you stop performing for others and start living for yourself.

But sometimes, without even realizing it, we carry old expectations with us. The "shoulds" we picked up over the years—how we're supposed to look, eat, move, or show up—don't just disappear. They become our inner voice. And suddenly, we're holding ourselves to standards we never actually chose in the first place.

Donna was one of those clients who showed up consistently but carried something heavy with her, something unspoken. She followed the workouts, did what I asked, but you could see it in her body language. She was hard on herself. Every movement felt like it had to be perfect. Every pause felt like failure.

She never said it outright, but it was clear: for Donna, being healthy meant being smaller. Her focus was always on shrinking, not strengthening. It was the mindset she'd been stuck in for years.

We never had a big, dramatic conversation about it. But during one of our sessions, I shifted the focus. I asked her to track how much stronger she was getting, not how much she weighed. We celebrated the reps she added. The way her posture changed. The moments she moved with more ease and less self-doubt.

And over time, I watched something shift.

She started smiling more in class. She moved with more ease. And one day, I noticed that she didn't even start her wearable. Instead of asking, "Did I burn enough calories?" she looked up with a grin and said, "I felt so strong today

That's the moment she stepped out of the old story. She stopped chasing someone else's version of success and started owning her own.

LETTING GO OF WHAT DOESN'T FIT ANYMORE ISN'T GIVING UP. IT'S GROWING INTO WHO YOU'RE MEANT TO BE.

That's what the expectation gap looks like. It's not always loud or dramatic. Sometimes, it's just a quiet moment where you decide: *I'm done living by someone else's rules.*

It shows up in small but powerful choices. Like choosing strength over the scale. Picking meals that leave you energized—not just the ones someone on Instagram says are "clean." Saying yes to rest, or joy, or time alone, even when others don't get it.

And when you start doing things differently—on your terms—that's when support becomes essential. Because going against the grain? It's not easy. You'll question yourself. You'll feel resistance. And some days, it'll feel like no one else gets it.

That's why having people in your corner matters. People who lift you up, who see your effort, who remind you that what you're doing *matters.*

Because real success isn't about fitting into someone else's mold. It's about creating a life that feels like home to *you.*

THE VISIBILITY GAP

Ever felt invisible? Unheard? Not acknowledged? That, my dear friend, is the visibility gap. It is the experience of feeling overlooked as if your presence, efforts, or ideas do not matter. Becoming more visible can profoundly affect confidence and how we present ourselves. It's about stepping out of the shadows and reclaiming your inner light.

Visibility comes in different forms. Speaking up in meetings, sharing your journey on social media, or simply wearing a bold new outfit. It's not just being seen. It's about feeling acknowledged and valued for the perspective you bring. When we feel heard and recognized, we can keep moving forward with our goals without feeling intimidated and instead feel confident.

For years, Eleanor struggled with feeling unseen. At family gatherings, conversations would flow around her, decisions were made without her input, and even when she tried to share her thoughts, they were often dismissed or ignored. It wasn't that people *meant* to exclude her. It was just the way things had always been. She had learned to stay quiet, not wanting to make waves.

One day, after yet another dinner where she barely spoke, she left feeling invisible, like she could've disappeared and no one would've noticed. That night, she promised herself she wouldn't keep playing small just to keep the peace.

So the next time the family gathered, she made a conscious effort to step into the conversation. She talked about her fitness journey, how she was learning to lift heavier weights, and how great it made her feel. At first, people barely reacted. But she kept going, refusing to shrink back. Because this time, she wasn't looking for approval, she was standing in her own power.

Then, something changed. Her sister asked a question about strength training. Her cousin chimed in about how she had always wanted to try lifting weights. For the first time, Eleanor was not just present. She was being heard.

This is the power of stepping into visibility. When we own our space and our experiences, we invite others to engage with us in a way they never have before.

Feeling seen and acknowledged can be a powerful force in staying committed to our health and fitness. When we stop fading into the background and start recognizing our worth, everything shifts. We fuel our bodies with care. We move with confidence. And we focus on our well-being, not for approval, but as a way to honor ourselves. Visibility isn't about attention, it's about presence. And when we choose to show up fully, we start living fully, too.

YOU DON'T NEED PERMISSION TO TAKE UP SPACE. YOU JUST NEED THE COURAGE TO STAY IN IT.

TAKE ACTION: CLOSING THE GAPS

We all experience gaps, moments where something feels missing. Confidence. Knowledge. Support. Realistic expectations. The feeling of being seen.

These gaps can leave us second-guessing, stuck, or silently wondering if change is even possible. But here's the truth: every gap has the same bridge and that is taking *action*.

Not a big, sweeping change. Just small, consistent, intentional steps.

Every time you choose to honor your body, speak up for yourself, ask for help, or try something new, you close that gap a little more. You don't need to have it all figured out. You just need to begin.

One step. One choice. One moment of courage at a time.

Ask yourself:

> " *Where do I feel stuck? Is it doubt, lack of knowledge, external expectations, or feeling unseen?*
> *What stories am I telling myself that keep me from moving forward?*
> *If I could approach this differently, what would that look like?* "

YOUR CHALLENGE

Choose *one* meaningful action that helps you move forward. Small steps lead to significant breakthroughs.

The more you recognize where these gaps show up, the more power you have to bridge them. Whether you ask for support, challenge a limiting belief, or take one small step toward your goal, you are in control.

Gaps look different for everyone. Some feel like small setbacks. Others feel impossible to cross. But they all have one thing in common, they hold us back. And if we're not careful, they lead us straight into the traps that keep us stuck.

Recognizing the gap is a start. But understanding *why* we keep falling into the same patterns? That's the key to breaking free.

Let's take a closer look at these traps so you can finally stop spinning your wheels and start moving forward.

CHAPTER 4

THE BIGGEST TRAPS

F eeling trapped doesn't always hit you all at once. Sometimes it sneaks up slowly.

For me, it started long before I realized it.

I never planned to marry or have children. That just wasn't the life I imagined for myself. My dream was to travel the world, live freely, untethered, chasing sunsets, not routines. I wanted adventure, not commitments.

But life has a funny way of surprising you.

I met Ken, my first husband, at a party during my first year in Washington, D.C. I didn't expect anything serious. We laughed. We danced. We talked for hours about everything and nothing. It felt light and fun. No pressure, no expectations, just ease.

And sometimes, that's how it starts. Not with a grand plan or a checklist, but with someone who feels familiar in all the right ways.

Then everything changed.

I got pregnant.

Suddenly, the adventurous life I had imagined disappeared. I left my job at the German Embassy. I became a mom. My world shrank to feedings, nap schedules, and household routines. Every financial decision had to be discussed. My partner, seventeen years older than me, was ready to settle down and talk about retirement. I felt like I was barely getting started.

I felt stuck. And for a long time, I ignored that feeling.

Until one day, I didn't.

I booked a trip to Germany, just me and the kids. No invite for him. When he asked why, the words came out before I even had time to think, "Because I want a divorce." I shocked even myself. I had never said those words out loud before, but the second they left my mouth, I knew. I had been holding that truth in for far too long. I didn't have a plan. I didn't have a financial safety net. I didn't even have the next step figured out. But I had something stronger: a deep, unshakable knowing that I couldn't keep living a life that didn't fit me anymore. It wasn't about being fearless, it was about being done. Done pretending. Done performing. Done staying stuck.

The next morning, everything looked the same, but nothing felt the same. The kitchen, the coffee mug in my hand, the sound of the kids in the background... all unchanged. But inside, something had shifted. I felt cracked wide open. Scared, yes. Alone, absolutely. But also... free. For the first time in years, I wasn't silencing myself. I didn't know how I was going to make it all work, but I knew I would. And that was enough to start over.

STARTING OVER

I took a full-time job as the Aerobics Director at the Aspen Hill Club in Silver Spring, Maryland. It wasn't glamorous, but it was mine. I had healthcare, paid vacation, a steady paycheck, and for the first time in years, a sense of control over my life. I was earning my own income, building a new foundation, and showing my kids what it looked like to choose yourself.

The divorce was hard. Starting over as a single mom was even harder. There were nights I lay awake wondering how I'd stretch one paycheck to cover everything, how I'd show up strong for my kids when I felt like I was falling apart. But something had shifted. I wasn't just surviving anymore. I was beginning to rebuild, brick by brick, choice by choice. And in the middle of all the uncertainty, I discovered a strength I didn't even know I had. Not the kind that needs applause, but the kind that's steady. The kind that rises with the alarm, makes the lunches, wipes the tears (sometimes my own), and keeps moving forward, because standing still was no longer an option.

At the time, I didn't have the language for what I was going through. I just knew I was stuck in a cycle, trying to hold it all together, trying to make things better, but always landing in the same place: tired, frustrated, and completely disconnected from the life I truly wanted.

That's what it feels like to be caught in a trap.
Maybe you've felt it too, an invisible net you're tangled in. Maybe you've told yourself, I'll deal with it later, but later keeps getting pushed down the road.

In this chapter, we're going to name these traps. The perfectionism. The all-or-nothing mindset. The guilt. The self-sabotage. All the subtle and not-so-subtle traps that keep you stuck, even when you're doing your best.

YOU CAN'T BREAK FREE FROM WHAT YOU DON'T SEE.

Because here's the truth most women don't talk about: we don't fall into these traps overnight. We slip into them little by little, in the moments when we say "yes" when we really meant "no," when we shrink to keep the peace, when we put our needs on hold just one more time. It happens in the spaces between what we want and what we allow, between what we need and what we keep giving away, between who we truly are and who we think we have to be.

Those spaces start out small, almost invisible. But if we don't pay attention, they slowly stretch and widen until they become the very traps that leave us stuck, exhausted, resentful, and wondering how we lost ourselves along the way. That's what we're diving into next.

WHY GAPS LEAD TO TRAPS

It doesn't happen all at once. Gaps form when we live out of alignment with what we truly need or want. Over time, those unaddressed gaps create patterns, ones that slowly pull us away from who we are until we no longer recognize the life we're living.

Tamara's Wake-Up Call
Remember my client Tamara? Tamara didn't even realize she was caught in a trap. She thought she was just doing what needed to be done, caring for her husband, running the household, handling the day-to-day. But over time, her spark faded. She had pushed her needs aside for so long that she didn't even notice how much of herself she had lost.

It wasn't until she told me, "Heike, I felt like myself again," that she saw just how far she had drifted from the woman she used to be. That moment wasn't about a fun weekend away. It was a wake-up call.

And that's the tricky thing about traps, they don't always look like obstacles. At first, they just feel like responsibility, routine, or being who others need you to be. But over time, they become cycles that secretly keep you stuck.

Gaps show up when there's a disconnect between what you truly want and how you're living day to day. When those gaps go unchecked, they harden into patterns. That's when they become traps, familiar routines that feel safe but keep you stuck in place.

These gaps don't just exist, they evolve. And if we're not paying attention, they slowly harden into habits, routines, and beliefs that keep us feeling stuck.

Let me show you what I mean.

THE HIDDEN WAYS GAPS BECOME TRAPS

Not Knowing Where to Start

Diane came to me frustrated. She wanted to improve her fitness but had no idea where to begin. She jumped into a random workout plan she found online, one designed for people way ahead of her in strength and endurance. Within weeks, she was burnt out, discouraged, and convinced that maybe she wasn't cut out for this.

What happened? Her gap in awareness led her straight into a trap of unrealistic expectations. Instead of choosing a path that fit her needs, she ended up chasing something that wasn't right for her. When it didn't work, she felt like she had failed.

Trying to Do Too Much at Once

Have you ever decided to "fix" everything at once? You commit to eating clean, working out five days a week, cutting out sugar, drinking more water, meditating, and getting eight hours of sleep, all starting Monday.

It feels exciting at first, but by midweek, you're exhausted, overwhelmed, and slipping back into old habits. That's because overwhelm itself is a trap, it convinces you that if you can't do everything, you might as well do nothing.

Sticking to What's Comfortable

Then there's the comfort zone. The place where things feel familiar, even if they're not working.

Take my client, Lisa. She loved running and had been doing it for years. But she kept getting injured, and her doctor suggested adding strength training. Even though she knew it could help, she hesitated. "I just don't feel comfortable in the weight room," she admitted.

She kept running, ignoring the growing pain in her knees, telling herself she was "staying active." The result? More injuries, more frustration, and a growing gap between what she needed and what she was actually doing.

Recognizing When You're Stuck

The truth is, we all have our own gaps and traps. Most of the time, we don't even see them until we're already caught in them. At first, they feel harmless. Familiar. Like part of our normal routine. But then, one day, we look around and realize we've been stuck in the same cycle for months… or even years.

Many of us have felt that sense of hitting a wall. We keep going, doing everything we're "supposed" to do, yet somehow still feel stuck, uninspired, or disconnected.

Maybe you've felt it, too. You wake up, go through the motions, check all the boxes…but deep down, something feels off. You're not miserable, but you're not exactly thriving either. You're doing enough, but are you truly living?

WHAT BEING STUCK CAN LOOK LIKE

You're Achieving…But It Feels Hollow

On paper, your life looks great. You've worked hard, checked off major milestones, and built something you're proud of. Yet every now and then, a question sneaks in: Is this all there is?

You can't quite put your finger on it, but something feels missing. A deeper purpose, a bigger adventure, or a shift that would make your success feel fuller. You don't know exactly what's next, but you feel a pull toward more.

Your Days Feel Like a Loop

Wake up. Go through the motions. End the day feeling... indifferent. Nothing is wrong, but nothing excites you either. Every day feels like a copy of the one before. You long for variety, spontaneity, or something fresh, yet you never actually make a change.

This isn't just boredom, it's a signal. You need a shift, a challenge, an adventure. Something to remind you what it feels like to be alive.

You Have "What If's" That Won't Go Away

What if I had taken that painting class? What if I had pursued that passion project? What if I had said yes instead of letting fear stop me?

These regrets aren't passing thoughts. They're reminders of what you still want for yourself. They show up again and again, nudging you, telling you that it's not too late.

You Crave Change...But Aren't Acting On It

You've been thinking about shaking things up. Trying something new. Finally going for it. But instead of taking action, you hesitate. You talk yourself out of it: It's too late... I don't have time... What if I fail?

You keep waiting for the "right time": I'll start when things settle down... maybe next year... after I lose the weight...

You watch others take bold steps and wonder why you can't seem to do the same. That longing? It's your inner self telling you that you're ready for more.

SO, WHAT'S STOPPING YOU?

This is the moment to pause and ask yourself: *What am I waiting for? What would happen if I took just one step forward today?*

If that question stirs something in you, you're not alone. Feelings like frustration, boredom, restlessness, even resignation and they're not random. They're signals. Signs that something needs to shift.

The truth is, many of us get caught in patterns we didn't even realize we were following. We repeat the same routines, think the same thoughts, and wonder why nothing's changing. That's where the traps come in.

THE 5 MOST COMMON TRAPS

Let's take a look at the five most common traps and how to finally break free.

TRAP #1: THE ALL-OR-NOTHING TRAP

Picture the world around us. It's like a pressure cooker, always focused on big wins, perfect scores, and flawless success stories. From media headlines to social feeds, we're constantly shown dramatic transformations, overnight achievements, and all-or-nothing thinking. The message is clear: if it's not done perfectly, it's not worth doing at all.

I learned this lesson early.

Growing up in my German household, perfection wasn't just encouraged, it was expected. A B- on a test didn't mean *good job*; it meant you could have done better. Maybe you know exactly what I'm talking about. Maybe you grew up hearing that if you're going to do something, you'd better do it right. That hard work is the only way to success. That if you can't give 100%, what's the point?

That kind of thinking doesn't just disappear. It follows us into midlife, especially when we're ready for change.

You wake up one day and think, *"Okay, time to get serious. I'm going to eat better, move more, and finally stick to it."*

YOU GO ALL IN. THE PERFECT PLAN. THE NEW GROCERY LIST. THE COLOR-CODED WORKOUTS.

But then life happens. You miss a workout. You eat something that wasn't "on plan." Suddenly that old voice sneaks in: *I blew it. I'll start over next week.*

That's the all-or-nothing trap. It convinces you that if it's not perfect, it's not worth doing. That unless you can give 100%, you might as well give up.

And that's what keeps so many women stuck, not because they can't follow through, but because doing it *imperfectly* feels like failure.

How many times have you hit pause on something, not because it wasn't working, but because it wasn't flawless? How often have you said, *"I'll wait until things settle down"* or *"I'll try again when I'm more motivated"*?

This trap isn't about discipline. It's about unrealistic expectations. And once you spot it, you can start choosing something better.

You don't need a perfect plan. You just need a doable one. Progress over perfection—every time.

TRAP #2: THE COMPARISON TRAP

Ever catch yourself thinking the grass is greener on someone else's side? Or feel that gut punch of envy when a friend shares a big win? You're not alone. That's the comparison trap, and we've all stepped into it.

Comparison is wired into us. From the time we're kids, we learn to measure ourselves against others. And that habit hasn't gone anywhere by the time we hit midlife. We look around—at careers, bodies, families, lifestyles—and wonder, am I doing enough? Am I falling behind?

But not all comparisons are bad. Sometimes, it sparks something.

Take my client Dora. She was in her mid-fifties when she noticed her neighbor training for a triathlon. At first, it was just admiration. Wow, I could never do that. But the more she watched her neighbor lace up her shoes, push through early morning workouts, and stick with it week after week, the more something shifted. A quiet tug started inside her. Not jealousy—curiosity. A whisper: I miss that feeling. I want to feel strong again.

She didn't sign up for a triathlon, but she did start walking longer distances, add strength training to her week, and try workouts she once assumed weren't for her. And she lit up, not because she was keeping up, but because she was reconnecting with her body, her energy, and her spark.

That's the power of positive comparison. It shows us what's possible. It helps us remember what we want.

But let's be real. Most of the time, comparison doesn't feel inspiring. It feels like a punch to the gut.

You finish a great workout, feeling proud, until you scroll through Instagram and see someone else running faster, lifting more, looking leaner. Suddenly, your win feels small. You were feeling confident. Now you're questioning everything.

It sneaks in everywhere. You notice your body has changed, and instead of grace, you compare it to how you looked ten years ago. You hear about someone else's promotion and wonder if you missed your chance. You watch families or relationships that seem picture-perfect and think, why not me?

These thoughts can spiral quickly. They don't just steal our joy, they distort our reality. They make us forget how far we've come. Instead of enjoying what we've built, they make us work harder to prove something.

The shift starts when you notice it. When you ask yourself, Is this comparison helping me or hurting me? Is it pointing me toward something I want, or pulling me away from who I am?

You don't need to erase the comparison. You just need to be in charge of it. Use it as a nudge, not a measuring stick.

You don't have to compete with anyone else's timeline. You get to define what success looks like in your life, your body, and your season.

That's where the real power lives, in coming home to yourself, again and again.

TRAP #3: THE PERFECTIONISM TRAP

Perfectionism sets us on a rocky path filled with intense emotions. It holds us back, keeping us from finishing things while convincing us that we aren't good enough. We feel stuck because nothing ever feels *done* or *perfect*.

Most people who struggle with perfectionism live in a cycle of constant stress and frustration. They redo things over and over, always feeling like they could have done better. Instead of feeling accomplished, they feel drained. Nothing ever meets the impossible standard they've set for themselves. That frustration turns inward, creating disappointment, anxiety, and self-doubt.

And then there's the hesitation.

You tell yourself you'll start once you're more prepared, when you have more time, when you can do it *right*. But days turn into weeks, weeks into months, and you're still waiting. Perfectionism convinces you that starting *imperfectly* is worse than not starting at all. If you *do* start, your focus is on what's *wrong*. Instead of celebrating progress, you pick apart every flaw.

When someone gives you feedback, maybe a coach, a friend, or even your own reflection, you don't hear advice; you hear confirmation that you're failing. Instead of seeing feedback as a tool for growth, it feels personal, like a spotlight shining on everything you're doing wrong.

Perfectionism keeps you trapped. It convinces you that mistakes mean you've failed when, in reality, they're just part of the process. You don't need to be *perfect* to move forward. You just need to start.

Recognizing these patterns is crucial. When you start seeing them for what they are, you can begin to question whether perfectionism is actually helping you or just holding you back.

A few years back, my client Pam sat across from me, frustration written all over her face.

"I don't get it," she sighed, shaking her head. "I've been doing everything right, but I still can't lose these last 10 pounds. What's the point if I'm not even getting results?"

She had followed her plan to the letter: counting every calorie, showing up to every workout, tracking every number. But if she slipped up, even a little? She felt like she had *ruined* everything. When we dug deeper, it became clear. Pam wasn't just frustrated with her weight. She was stuck in the perfectionism trap. Somewhere along the way, she had convinced herself that unless everything was perfect, her efforts didn't count. If she wasn't hitting the number on the scale she had set in her head, none of it mattered.

"I just need to get back to my high school weight," she admitted, almost embarrassed to say it out loud.

I could see how much pressure she was putting on herself. So I asked her a different question.

"What if we stopped focusing on a number on the scale? What if, instead, we looked at what your body can do?"

She paused. At first, the idea of letting go of the number felt like giving up. For years, that goal had given her something to measure. Something to chase. But deep down, she was tired. Tired of doing everything "right" and still feeling like she was failing. Tired of never feeling good enough.

And in that exhaustion, something shifted. She didn't want to keep beating herself up. She wanted a break from the pressure. A life that felt lighter. More doable. Less about chasing perfection and more about feeling good in her skin.

She didn't leap into it. But she leaned in. Slowly, she began shifting her attention from the number on the scale to the strength in her legs—legs that let her hike through the mountains with her husband, tend her garden, and chase her grandkids. She started noticing how her body supported her life, not just how it looked. And with every small mindset shift, she felt a little more free.

The pressure to be perfect began to loosen its grip. She stopped labeling every meal as "good" or "bad." She moved because it felt good, not because she had to earn her next meal. And for the first time in years, she began to feel at ease in her body.

Perfectionism convinces us that only flawless effort counts. That if we can't do it exactly right, we shouldn't do it at all. But growth doesn't happen in perfect conditions—it happens in motion. It happens when we show up, stumble, adjust, and keep going anyway. Progress isn't about doing it all. It's about doing *something*. And the moment we stop striving for perfection and start choosing progress, we begin to move forward.

TRAP #4: THE "NOT ENOUGH TIME" TRAP

This trap convinces us that we have to earn our worth through constant doing and that there's never enough time to get it all done. The day slips by, and somehow the things we *want* most—movement, rest, creativity, connection—always end up last on the list.

For midlife women, this is especially common. We spend years putting everyone else first, and somewhere along the way, we start believing there's simply no room left for ourselves.

But here's the truth: it's often not about time. It's about permission. Permission to prioritize your needs. To say no without guilt. To stop proving your value by how much you can juggle.

Once we shift how we see time, not as something we have to earn, but something we get to reclaim and we start to break free from this trap.

Where Does The Time Go?

We've all said it: *"There's just not enough time in the day."* Work drains your energy with emails, meetings, and deadlines, leaving you too exhausted to do anything else, even the things meant to recharge you.

Then come the social obligations. Events you didn't really want to attend. Favors you agreed to out of habit. You can't remember when you said yes, but now your calendar is full and your own priorities have been pushed to "maybe tomorrow."

But then tomorrow comes... and looks exactly the same.

Perfectionism doesn't help either. That email you keep tweaking, the task you overthink, the organizing that turns into procrastination, it all adds up. And before you know it, another hour is gone.

Time isn't just slipping away. It's being given away. Bit by bit, choice by choice.

Why This Trap Feels So Hard to Escape

The "Not Enough Time" trap makes it feel like life is happening *to* you, like you're just trying to stay afloat. And making time for yourself? That can feel selfish or downright impossible.

But here's a reframe: time isn't something you *find*. It's something you *reclaim*.

Ask yourself:

> **"** *How often do you say yes when you really want to say no?*
> *How often do you chase perfect when "done"*
> *would be just fine?*
> *When was the last time you did something just for you—*
> *without guilt?* **"**

Recognizing these patterns isn't a sign you're failing. It's a sign you're waking up. And that's the first step toward taking your time and your power back.

But even when we start reclaiming our time, there's another trap waiting: the one where we get in our own way. Not because we can't do it, but because deep down, a part of us is afraid of what happens if we actually succeed.

TRAP #5: THE SELF-SABOTAGE TRAP

It's frustrating, isn't it? You set a goal. You make a plan. You tell yourself *this time* will be different. And yet somehow, you find yourself slipping back, almost without realizing it, into old habits.

You swear you'll stick to your workout schedule, but the couch feels more inviting after a long day. You plan to eat healthier, yet suddenly, there's a bag of chips in your cart instead of the meal-prep ingredients you meant to buy. You tell yourself you'll finally carve out time for yourself, only to fill that time with everyone else. It doesn't make sense. You *want* to change. You've read the articles. You've tried the plans. You've told yourself, *This time, I'll stick with it.* So why does it still feel like you're the one standing in your own way?

That's self-sabotage. And the worst part? Most of the time, we don't even realize we're doing it. There's always someone who needs us, something urgent pulling our attention. And somewhere in all that noise, we convince ourselves that our needs can wait.

But that's not the only way we sabotage ourselves.

Sometimes it's not about being too busy, it's about telling ourselves stories that keep us small. *Maybe I don't really need this. Maybe I'm fine just the way things are.* And just like that, we let ourselves off the hook. We retreat into comfort, even when a part of us is quietly craving more.

Self-sabotage doesn't always look like making the "wrong" choice. More often, it's the subtle way we avoid the right one.

It's filling your only free hour with scrolling, not because you're lazy, but because you're afraid of failing—again. It's signing up for the class, then backing out with what feels like a totally valid excuse. *I'm too busy. It's too expensive. I'll start next month.* It's sneaky. And it happens all the time.

But why though?
Because deep down, change threatens your comfort. Even if that comfort isn't working for you anymore, it's familiar and the familiar feels safe. Self-sabotage is often a form of self-protection. If you don't try, you can't fail. If you don't begin, you don't risk becoming someone new.

But staying stuck has a cost, too.

The Hidden Reasons Behind Self-Sabotage
So, why do we do this?

Because real change, lasting change, is uncomfortable. Even when we deeply want it, a part of us resists. Sometimes, that resistance is loud. More often, it's quiet and convincing.

Here's what it can look like:

Fear of failure. What if you try and it doesn't work? What if you give it your all and still don't succeed? Rather than risk that disappointment, it feels safer not to try at all.

Fear of success. It sounds strange, but success means change. And change is scary. It means stepping into a new version of yourself, and that can be unsettling. Who will you be if you actually reach your goal? What will it mean for your relationships, your routines, your life?

Low self-esteem. Deep down, you might question whether you truly deserve success. After years of putting yourself last, it's easy to believe this is just how things are supposed to be.

Comfort in the familiar. Even if you're unhappy where you are, it feels familiar. And the familiar feels safer than the unknown, even if the unknown holds the life you want.

Unresolved emotions. Past failures, disappointments, or stories you've carried for years can create invisible walls. You might say you're ready, but part of you is still holding back.

Autopilot patterns. Self-sabotage is not always a conscious decision. Often, it's just the default. Habits and behaviors you've repeated so many times, you don't even realize you're doing them.

Take Beth, for example. She's been trying to carve out time for herself, planning to start a morning routine, including a workout and quiet time before the day got busy. But every night, a friend would call and vent about her problems. Beth would stay on the phone late, offering advice and emotional support, telling herself it was the right thing to do.

By morning, she's exhausted. Her plans to take care of herself keep getting pushed aside, not because she didn't want to prioritize herself, but because she never says no to others.

Over time, always saying yes to others became its form of self-sabotage. She didn't realize it, but by constantly showing up for everyone else, she had slowly stopped showing up for herself.

And that's exactly how this trap works: the more we delay our needs, the easier it becomes to forget them.

So what's the missing piece?

Boundaries.

Not walls. Not ultimatums. Boundaries are how we care for ourselves while still caring for others. They're how we reclaim the time, energy, and space we need to grow.

And that's exactly what we're going to dive into next.

SETTING BOUNDARIES

My client Tanja had always been the go-to person in her family, the one who handled everything. So when her elderly mother needed more care, moving her into her home seemed like the natural choice.

At first, Tanja told herself it was temporary, just until they figured out a long-term plan. But weeks turned into months, and before she knew it, her mother had taken over her life and her home. Her days were dictated by her mother's needs. Doctor's appointments, meal prep, and errands were all on her shoulders.

Her husband? They barely had time together. Her grown children? She missed their calls and events because she was always too busy.

But the hardest part? Her mother didn't see it as a problem. She expected Tanja to always be available, to drop everything at a moment's notice. And when Tanja finally carved out a rare moment for herself, her mother would call, interrupt, or guilt her for not being there.

One day, as she sat in the doctor's office with her mother yet again, she had a moment of clarity. She had set any boundaries. Not with her mom. Not with herself. Her home was not hers anymore. And Tanja realized if she did not change something, her life would not be hers anymore either.

That night, she sat down with her husband and made a decision. It was time to set boundaries.

It wasn't easy, so she started small. She set specific hours where she was available for her mother and stuck to them. She reclaimed parts of her home for herself and her family, creating space where she could be "off duty." She said, "Not right now mom," to non emergencies, reminding herself that being a good daughter did not mean being on call 24/7.

At first, her mother pushed back. She tested every boundary, guilt-tripping Tanja and trying to pull her back into old patterns. And for a moment, Tanja almost gave in. That familiar pull, the fear of letting someone down was strong.

But this time, she didn't.

And something unexpected happened.

Tanja began to feel like herself again. She went on long walks with her husband, without rushing. She sat at the dinner table with her kids, actually present. She finally signed up for the class she'd been thinking about for years, not because she had to, but because she wanted to.

That's when she realized boundaries weren't about shutting others out. They were about finally showing up for herself.

Because here's the truth: the world will always ask more of you. But you don't have to give away your energy, your time, or your joy just to keep up. You're allowed to take up space in your own life.

HOW BOUNDARIES SET YOU FREE

Boundaries aren't about cutting people off, they're about choosing to include yourself. They're how you protect your energy, your time, and your well-being. They help you stop running on empty and start honoring what matters to *you*.

Because here's the truth: if you don't set boundaries, someone else will set them for you. And when you're always rearranging your life around everyone else's needs, your own identity starts to fade, just like Tanja experienced.

BREAKING FREE STARTS HERE

Boundaries are only the beginning. The real freedom comes when you start shifting the patterns that kept you stuck in the first place. And that shift doesn't require a complete life overhaul. It starts with one honest moment.

What are you still holding onto that no longer serves you?
Which trap do you find yourself slipping into again and again?
What's one small act of self-respect you can take today?

Pause. Reflect. This is your moment.
Awareness opens the door. Now it's your turn to walk through it.

TAKE ACTION

You've just unpacked some of the most common traps that keep midlife women stuck. And maybe, for the first time, you see your own patterns more clearly. That's a powerful first step, but awareness alone won't move you forward.

Now it's time to shift from reflection into action.

Ask yourself:

> **"**
>
> *What trap am I still holding onto?*
> *Is it perfectionism? Comparison? Overwhelm? Self-sabotage?*
> *What's one simple thing I can do this week*
> *to shift that pattern?*
>
> **"**

Be honest. Name it. Write it down.

> *Example:* I used to fall hard into the perfectionism trap. I believed if something wasn't done perfectly, it wasn't worth doing at all. So I'd stall, waiting for the perfect time, the perfect plan, or the perfect circumstances. But all that waiting only kept me stuck. Once I gave myself permission to start messy, everything changed. Action, not perfection is what got me unstuck.

Your turn.

Write down the trap that's been keeping you stuck.

Then ask: *What's one thing I can do this week to shift it?*

It might be setting a boundary. It might be asking for help. It might be giving yourself permission to rest.

KEEP IT SIMPLE. SMALL STEPS CREATE MOMENTUM AND MOMENTUM IS WHAT GETS YOU UNSTUCK.

RECLAIM YOUR SPARK

You've started to see the traps. You've reflected, questioned, and maybe even named the patterns that have been holding you back.

So now what?

When you say, "I just want to feel like myself again", what you're really saying is:

"
"I'm tired of holding back."
"I want my energy back."
"I want to feel strong, confident, and actually enjoy my life." **"**

But somewhere along the way, life took over. You woke up with the best intentions… only to have your day swallowed by deadlines, family needs, errands, and responsibilities. Everyone else came first. And little by little, without even realizing it, you started fading into the background.

Maybe you stopped moving the way you used to. Maybe your confidence took a hit. Maybe some days, you look in the mirror and barely recognize the woman staring back.

It's not that you stopped caring. You care deeply. But finding the energy to make a change? That part feels harder to reach.

PURSUE YOUR SPARK

Here's what I want you to know: **Your spark isn't gone. It's not lost. It's just been buried under everything life has asked of you.**

You don't need to fix yourself, because you were never broken. What you need is a way back. A path to reconnect with the part of you that's still hungry for more. The part that knows there's still something waiting.

That's what the SPARK Framework is here for.

Not to take you backward, but to help you move forward into the version of you that feels strong, clear, and fully alive in this season of life.

Because you're not done. Not even close.

There's more strength to build. Confidence to grow. Joy to feel. And the best part? You don't have to figure it out alone.

WHAT'S NEXT: THE WAY BACK TO YOU

You've named the traps. You've spotted the patterns. Now it's time to shift from stuck to forward.

Not by doing everything at once, but by taking one doable step at a time with a framework that works in real life, not just on paper.

That's exactly what the SPARK path will guide you through and I'll be right here walking it with you.

CHAPTER 5

HOW TO FEEL LIKE YOURSELF AGAIN

My kids were three and seven when I chose to leave my marriage. I didn't have a financial safety net. No clear plan. Just the unshakable truth that staying was no longer an option—and that somehow, I'd figure the rest out.

I still remember standing in the kitchen, gripping the edge of the counter, heart pounding. The walls felt like they were closing in. The life I had built didn't feel like mine anymore. I had two choices: stay in a life where I felt invisible or step into the unknown.

With shaking hands, I chose the unknown and walked away.

Fortunately, with the support of a friend, that lifeline we all need, I found a small townhouse to rent. My co-workers helped me move in, carrying the few pieces of furniture I had left after the divorce. My ex-husband had paid for the house we used to live in, and now, for the first time, I was staring down rent, food, school supplies, and everything else on my own.

I was proud of my growing fitness career, but pride couldn't pay the bills.

The townhouse wasn't much, but it was mine. It smelled like fresh paint and possibility. Every step echoed on the bare floors, a reminder of how little I brought with me. But then I unfolded a chair, sat down by the window, and let out a breath I didn't know I'd been holding.

This is mine, I thought. *This is where I begin again.*

Just when I needed it most, something unexpected happened.

Lisa, an aerobics teacher at a large health club, decided to leave her position and on her way out, she recommended me to the managers. That one gesture changed everything.

Almost overnight, I had something stable: full-time hours, childcare when the kids weren't in school, a steady paycheck, and the chance to earn extra income through personal training. They hired me almost on the spot.

It was a lifeline I never saw coming and for the first time in a long time, I felt like I was finding my footing again. I wasn't just surviving. The path had appeared.

But stepping into this new chapter wasn't just about the paycheck. It was about coming back to myself.

Managing a team of 34 instructors, coordinating class schedules, and juggling life as a single mom, it was exciting, but it was also overwhelming. I remember one morning when my youngest woke up with a fever. Panic surged through me. Do I call in and risk losing the job that's keeping us afloat? Or do I leave my sick child with a neighbor and hope for the best?

The weight of single motherhood pressed on my chest. No matter what I chose, I felt like I was letting someone down.

I *had* to learn to set boundaries. My club manager didn't care how I handled childcare or sick days as long as I showed up. I wanted to be loyal to my job, but I had to be loyal to myself and my kids first.

One evening after putting the kids to bed, I sat at the kitchen table. I stared at the calendar filled with meetings, classes, and school events. For the first time in a long time, I didn't feel like I was surviving. I was steering the ship. I had built this life from scratch. And while it was messy and exhausting, it was mine.

The gap between my old life and my new one felt vast, uncertain, and at times impossible to cross. But I knew I couldn't let fear keep me standing still. Moving forward meant choosing progress over perfection and trusting that even the smallest steps were taking me somewhere.

With support, with work, and with a whole lot of faith, I wasn't just finding myself again. I was becoming the woman I was always meant to be.

LAYING THE FOUNDATION FOR CHANGE

By now, you've likely recognized a gap or two in your life and a few traps that may keep you stuck. But it's not enough to see them. Now we've got to break free from those traps and start building the life we've always dreamed of. This is where you begin to clarify what you really want and take steps toward it in a way that feels realistic, empowering, and sustainable.

Soon, we'll dive into the SPARK Framework, where you'll get the simple strategies to turn those goals into real momentum.

WHY NOW? WHY NOT LATER?

It's tempting to stay where you are, even when it's not where you truly want to be. Because let's be honest: change is uncomfortable. The unknown can feel overwhelming. But waiting won't make it easier. And it won't make you feel more ready.

PURSUE YOUR SPARK

This isn't about becoming someone else. It's about coming back to *you*—your confidence, your energy, your sense of purpose.

If you're still reading this, it's not a coincidence. Some part of you is ready. Ready to stop spinning your wheels. Ready to feel alive again.

You don't need to overhaul your life overnight. You just need to take the next right step. Small, manageable actions, that's what creates momentum. And that momentum? It changes everything.

Because the truth is: staying stuck might feel familiar, but it won't move you forward. Starting—*even imperfectly*—is what will.

Your health is your greatest asset, the foundation for everything else. Without it, enjoying time with family, pursuing your passions, or simply feeling good each day becomes harder. Taking action now is an investment in your future self, so you can move through the years ahead with strength, energy, and purpose.

The longer you wait, the wider the gap becomes. That space between where you are and where you want to be starts to feel overwhelming. But the moment you take that first step, you begin to close it.

Progress doesn't happen all at once. It's not about crossing the finish line overnight, it's about choosing to move forward, one decision at a time.

And here's the most important part: **you don't have to do this alone**.

Yes, this journey is personal. But that doesn't mean you have to figure it out by yourself. That's why this book exists, to walk beside you.

Through the SPARK Framework, you'll uncover a clear, doable path forward. You'll also meet Emma, Lisa and Jasmine, three women just like you, who put these steps into action in their lives. Their stories will show you that there's no one right way to change, just your way. Small steps, taken with intention, can lead to powerful transformations.

YOUR FIRST STEP

Reclaiming your spark starts with awareness. Before we get into the how, take a moment to check in with where you are, so you can move forward with clarity and purpose.

Ask yourself: *How do I want to feel moving forward?*
Not what you want to fix, and not what you wish looked different, but how you genuinely want to feel in your daily life.

Maybe it's energized, empowered, calm, confident, or more connected to your body. Close your eyes and imagine what that would feel like for you.

For example, you might write: *I want to wake up with more energy, feel strong in my body, and stop feeling like I'm always behind.*
Once you're clear on how you want to feel, it becomes easier to make choices that support that feeling, instead of reacting to pressure or other people's expectations.

To help anchor this, choose three words that describe how you want to feel over the next 30 days. Words like **energized, grounded, strong.** Or maybe it's **calm, focused, free.** Pick what resonates with *you.*

Write them down and put them somewhere you'll see often—on your mirror, in your journal, or as a reminder on your phone

Then ask yourself:
What's one small daily habit that would support that feeling?
Just one.
Start there. That's your first spark.

WHAT IS THE SPARK FRAMEWORK?

It's the way you start creating a life that feels energizing, meaningful, and right for *you*.

It was built with midlife women in mind, especially those who feel stuck, stretched too thin, or just tired of putting themselves last. If you're ready to take small, doable steps that lead to real change, you're in the right place.

In the chapters ahead, we'll walk through each part of the SPARK Framework, step by step. You'll get clear on where you are right now, what matters most to you, and how to move forward in a way that actually fits your life (not someone else's idea of what it *should* look like).

This isn't about perfection. It's not about overhauling your life overnight. It's about taking intentional steps that build momentum and keep you moving, even when life gets messy.

You won't be doing this alone. You'll have support, stories, and practical tools to help you along the way. And you'll learn how to navigate those roadblocks that used to stop you, not by powering through, but by approaching them differently.

You're not here by accident. You're here because something inside you is ready for more.

So let's begin. Step by step, we'll create change that makes a difference in your life.

THE FIVE STEPS OF THE SPARK FRAMEWORK

The SPARK Framework is made up of five simple steps that help you get clear, take action, and build momentum. Each one focuses on a different part of your life, your mindset, your habits, your energy and together, they help you move forward in a way that feels doable. It's not about doing everything at once. It's about making small changes that actually stick and feeling the difference as you go.

Here's how each part of SPARK will help guide your next steps:

S - Self-Assessment
We'll start by taking an honest look at where you are right now, your health, your mindset, your habits. No judgment. Just awareness. This gives us the foundation we need to move forward with intention.

P - Planning Your Path
Once you know where you are, you can start mapping out where you want to go. We're not talking about big, lofty goals that don't fit your life. We're talking about a realistic path, one that actually works with your time, your energy, and your priorities.

A- Action Toward Goals
This is where things start to shift. You'll take simple, consistent actions that move you forward. No more all-or-nothing. Just doable steps that add up.

R - Recognizing Obstacles
Life's going to throw you curveballs. But instead of getting knocked off track, you'll start noticing the patterns and roadblocks that trip you up and learn how to work around them without losing momentum.

K - Keeping Momentum
This is about staying with it. Not with hustle or burnout, but with strategies that help you stay energized, motivated, and connected to why you started in the first place.

By following these five steps, you're not chasing some perfect version of yourself. You're building a life that actually fits—one that feels strong, steady, and fulfilling. This isn't about quick fixes. It's about making real changes that stick and finally feeling like yourself again.

FROM STUCK TO STARTING

You don't need to figure everything out today. Just by recognizing where you feel stuck, you've already taken the first step.

This book is here to help you keep moving forward, with tools, strategies, and stories that meet you where you are. The SPARK Framework isn't a rigid plan. It's flexible and built to work with real life. You can move through each step at your own pace, revisit sections when you need a reset, or focus on one area that feels most relevant right now.

Whether you're just getting started or ready to level up, this is your space to reflect, take action, and grow in a way that feels aligned with your life, not someone else's version of success.

In the next chapters, we'll break down each SPARK step into practical, doable actions—so you can start rebuilding your energy, confidence, and strength, one step at a time.

IGNITE YOUR SPARK

Now that you've been introduced to the SPARK Framework, let it settle in for a moment. It's a powerful guide, but more than that, it's your next step toward creating a life that actually feels like yours again.

You might feel a mix of excitement and uncertainty. That's normal. This kind of change isn't about rushing in or getting it perfect, it's about starting where you are, with what you have.

And that's exactly what Ann did.

She was used to going all in: strict routines, rigid plans, high expectations. But every time life got busy, work deadlines, family responsibilities, her progress disappeared. The cycle was exhausting.

After joining the *Pursue Your Spark Blueprint*, she let go of the pressure to do everything at once. She slowed down. She focused on one small change at a time.

At first, it felt unfamiliar. But as she let go of the all-or-nothing mindset, she noticed something: *these small steps stuck.* She stopped starting over. She began building something that lasted.

"The course taught me that small, incremental steps can lead to significant, lasting changes. This mindset shift was a game-changer for me."

Ann's story is a reminder that real transformation doesn't come from perfection, but it comes from consistency, compassion, and showing up for yourself even when it's not ideal.

Now, it's your turn.
Take a moment to reflect: Which part of SPARK feels most relevant to where you are today?

 Maybe you're craving clarity and can't wait to dive into Self-Assessment.
Maybe Recognizing Obstacles speaks to you because you're tired of pushing through without pausing.

PURSUE YOUR SPARK

There's no wrong answer, just pay attention to what pulls at you.

If you want, jot it down. Use a journal or the worksheets linked through the QR code at the beginning of this book to keep track of what stands out. This doesn't have to be linear. Start where you are. Come back when you need a reset. Move forward when you feel ready.

We'll focus on mindset, fitness, and nutrition, three key areas that work together to help you feel strong, clear, and energized.

Whether you're ready to dive in or just starting to explore, this is your journey. Go at your pace. Remember: Small steps lead to big change.

You've got this!

CHAPTER 6

SELF-ASSESSMENT

WHY SELF-ASSESSMENT MATTERS

Before you can move forward, you need to know where you're starting from.

That's what self-assessment is about, not judgment, not perfection, but awareness. It's how you start making choices that actually move you in the direction you want to go.

Because if you've ever thought, "I should have this figured out by now," or "Why does this feel so hard?" You're not alone. That stuck feeling isn't because you're not trying hard enough. It's because you haven't had a clear view of where you are.

Real change doesn't come from doing more. It comes from understanding what you need right now, so that your next steps actually lead somewhere.

Maybe you've started workouts before, only to stop after a few weeks. Maybe you've changed your eating habits, but slipped back into old routines. Or maybe, no matter how hard you try, it still feels like something's missing.

That's not because you've failed. It's because without a clear understanding of where you're starting from, it's easy to fall into the same patterns, trying different things, hoping something sticks.

When you step back and look at the full picture, your mindset, your movement, your nutrition, you start to see what's really going on. That clarity makes everything easier. Your next steps finally have direction and purpose.

Self-assessment isn't about getting it perfect. It's about spotting what's working, what's not, and what needs attention. That's why we start with mindset in the SPARK Framework, because the way you think drives everything else.

You don't need to have it all figured out. You just need to be honest about where you are. That's the first real step toward change that actually sticks.

MINDSET: HOW YOU THINK SHAPES EVERYTHING

When my husband Jan gave me a saxophone, he wasn't trying to challenge me. He just remembered something I'd once said in passing, that if I ever learned to play an instrument, it would be the saxophone.

I have no formal music training. No big plan to become great. Just a wish I had carried for years… and now, here it was, sitting in my hands.

I didn't feel "ready." I didn't have it all figured out. But I did have something else—curiosity. And that was enough to begin. One small, squeaky note at a time.

That's the power of a growth mindset. It's not about being perfect. It's about being open. Open to trying. Open to learning. Open to doing something simply because it matters to *you*.

So what about you?

When something new calls to you, do you follow it? Or do you shut it down before you even begin?

FITNESS: WHERE ARE YOU NOW?

You don't need to run marathons or have a perfect routine to take your fitness seriously. You just need to know where you're starting from.

Progress doesn't come from pushing harder, it comes from getting honest. Honest about how you feel right now, what your body needs, and what's actually doable in this season of life.

I've been at peak fitness, and I've had to rebuild from scratch more times than I can count. And what I've learned is this: your body will meet you where you are—if you show up for it.

This isn't about doing more. It's about reconnecting with what strong feels like *for you*—right now.

Quick Fitness Self-Check
Let's get a clear picture of where you are right now, no judgment, just honest reflection.

On a scale of 1 to 5, how would you rate your current fitness level?
(1 = I feel out of shape and low on energy, 5 = I feel strong, consistent, and energized in my routine)

Now take it a step deeper:

- What types of movement feel good in my body right now?
- Are there any that feel out of reach or intimidating?
- What fitness habits have I been consistent with—*even in small ways?*
- Where do I feel strong?
- Where have I lost momentum?

This isn't about grading yourself. It's about noticing what's working and what needs more support. Once you see it, you can start moving forward with clarity.

NUTRITION: MAKING IT WORK FOR YOU

I've been cooking since I was a teen, but my relationship with food has changed many times over the years. Early on, it was all about what was quick, affordable, and filling—whatever got the job done. Later, I started to see how food could actually support my energy, my mood, and my overall well-being.

It wasn't about following strict rules. It was about learning what worked for *me.*

Now take a moment to look at your own eating and cooking habits—not through the lens of "good" or "bad," but through curiosity.

- What kinds of meals make you feel your best—energized, satisfied, steady?
- Are there times of day when you tend to skip meals, overeat, or feel drained?
- Do you feel stuck in a rut with cooking or unsure what to make?
- What's working in your current routine—and what's not?

This isn't about a perfect diet. It's about understanding how food fits into your life right now—and how to make it work *for* you, not against you.

Reflect on the following:
- What are some of your favorite foods or go-to meals? What do you love about them?
- When you hear the phrase *"healthy eating,"* what does that mean to you—realistically?
- What's your biggest challenge when it comes to eating in a way that feels good and sustainable?
- On a scale from 1 to 5, how would you rate your current relationship with food?
  (1 = "I dread it," 5 = "I look forward to meals and feel at ease with food")

This isn't about changing your habits—yet. It's about seeing your patterns clearly, so you can work with them, not against them.

MINDSET AND ENDURANCE ARE AS IMPORTANT AS PHYSICAL ABILITY IN ACHIEVING SUCCESS.

TAKE ACTION: START SMALL, START REAL

You've taken an honest look at your mindset, fitness, and nutrition—what's working, what's not, and where you might be stuck. Now it's time to take that insight and turn it into movement.

Not a complete overhaul. Not a 10-step plan. Just one small, doable step forward—something that actually fits your life right now.

Here's how to get started:

STEP 1: NAME WHAT'S HOLDING YOU BACK

Take a moment to ask yourself: *What's been getting in the way lately? Is it a lack of time? Feeling overwhelmed? Not knowing where to start?*

You don't need to fix it all right now, just name it.

And if you can't quite put your finger on it, start writing whatever comes to mind without filtering or censoring. That's where change begins..

STEP 2: CHOOSE ONE FOCUS AREA

Now that you've named the challenge, choose one area—mindset, fitness, or nutrition—that feels ready for a shift. Then, pick *one* small action to support it.

Maybe it's going for a walk three times this week, journaling in the morning, or prepping a healthy snack. Keep it simple. Keep it realistic.

STEP 3: LET SOMEONE IN

Think of one person who supports you and let them know what you're working on.

You don't have to ask for anything big, just share your goal. Having someone in your corner can make all the difference.

STEP 4: KEEP TRACK IN A WAY THAT FEELS NATURAL

Tracking doesn't have to be fancy. Maybe you jot a quick note in your calendar, leave a sticky on the fridge, or do a one-minute check-in before bed.

The goal is to *notice your effort* and let that build momentum.

STEP 5: STAY FLEXIBLE

Life will throw curveballs. That's okay. If your plan doesn't happen today, ask:

What's one small way I can still show up for myself?

Flexibility is what keeps you moving forward, especially when things don't go perfectly.

You don't have to do it all. You just have to begin. Choose one small step, take it this week, and trust that it counts, because it does.

You've already done the hardest part: getting clear.

You've looked at where you are, what's working, and what's not. That kind of honesty gives you the clarity to move forward with purpose.

Now comes the empowering part: deciding what's next.

CASE STUDIES

As we move through the SPARK Framework, you'll meet three women—Emma, Lisa, and Jasmine—each with different stories, struggles, and goals.

You might see parts of yourself in them: feeling stuck, craving change, wanting to feel strong and feel like yourself again.

Their journeys will show you how this framework can look in real life and remind you that you're not alone in figuring it out.

CASE STUDY #1: EMMA

52 years old | Busy Professional | Family-Focused | Fitness Beginner

Emma is 52, working full-time as an office manager while juggling family life and caregiving for her aging parents. Everyone counts on her, but she stopped counting on herself somewhere along the way.

She was constantly tired, and her body felt heavier. Even the smallest changes, like walking upstairs or choosing what to eat, felt harder than they used to. She wasn't unhappy exactly, just...worn down. She didn't feel like herself.

The hardest part? Making time. Emma was always last on her list. Something else always felt more urgent, even when she wanted to make changes. And on the rare days when she *tried to start something new, the pressure to get it all right would stop her before she* got going.

At first, she thought, "What's the point? I'll never stick with it." But something needed to shift. So she started small, with a 20-minute walk after dinner. Just that one thing. It didn't fix everything, but gave her something she hadn't had in a long time: a sense of ownership over her day.

From there, she started keeping a simple journal of what she ate and how it made her feel. There were no rules, no tracking apps, just patterns. She noticed that skipping meals left her drained and that her go-to snacks gave her a short boost, then a crash. With that awareness, she began to swap in a few easy, nourishing choices: more water, fresh fruit, and a veggie with dinner.

Each step gave her a bit more energy, clarity, and belief in herself.

Emma didn't do it all at once. She didn't need to. What she needed was a starting point, a plan she could actually live with, and the confidence to trust that it was enough.

CASE STUDY #2: LISA

Marketing Director | Health-Savvy but Overwhelmed | On-Again, Off-Again with Fitness

Lisa, 48, works in a high-pressure marketing role and is the kind of woman who gets things done. She knows what healthy habits look like. She's had seasons where she was on fire, riding her bike regularly, lifting weights, and meal prepping like a pro, but that momentum never lasted.

Every time life got a little hectic, her routines unraveled. One week off turned into two, and she'd lost the rhythm completely before long. The biggest challenge wasn't knowing what to do—it was *sticking with it*.

So we started small.

Lisa picked one non-negotiable: a Saturday morning workout she could commit to no matter what her week looked like. That one habit gave her a sense of consistency, something she could trust, even when the rest of life felt unpredictable. It grounded her.

Meal prep was another sticking point. Lisa didn't need a new diet; she needed something she could lean on during her busiest days. So she blocked off one hour on Sundays, just enough to prep a few grab-and-go meals and snacks. It was not perfect, not elaborate, but it took the pressure off during the week and kept her from defaulting to takeout or convenience food.

The most significant shift came in how she handled setbacks. Before, one skipped workout or "off-plan" meal would send her into guilt mode, followed by quitting altogether. Now? She's learning to reset without the drama. A walk, a balanced dinner, a moment to reflect. Instead of spiraling, she simply begins again.

Lisa's story is about learning to *stay in the game*—not perfectly, not rigidly, but with enough consistency and compassion to keep moving forward—especially on the days that feel off-track.

CASE STUDY #3: JASMINE

Retired Executive | Lifelong Athlete | Evolving Her Purpose

At 61, Jasmine is the kind of woman who walks into a room and people notice. Not just because she's strong, but because she radiates confidence, clarity, and presence. Fitness isn't new for her—it's a lifelong companion. She's run marathons, competed in local fitness challenges, and has a fridge that looks like a nutritionist's dream.

But recently, Jasmine has felt a shift. She's not slowing down, but something inside her asks a different question: *What's next?*

Her routines are solid. Her motivation is still there. But she's starting to notice the edges. The recovery takes longer. The results aren't as fast. And if she's honest, some days feel more like maintenance than momentum. That sense of forward motion she's always chased? It's harder to find.

So, instead of doubling down, Jasmine decides to pull back—in a different way. She starts exploring new strategies centered not on effort but on recovery: better sleep, more mobility, slower mornings, and stress management. She's learning that her next level doesn't come from doing more but from doing what matters *smarter*.

She also shakes up her routine. Pilates-based strength work, mindful movement, and flexibility training become new forms of challenge, not because they're easy but because they're unfamiliar. They demand a different kind of strength and focus, and that lights her up again.

Perhaps the most significant shift for Jasmine isn't physical. Its purpose. She's been doing this for decades, and now she's feeling a pull to give back. To mentor. To guide. To help other women see what's possible—not by preaching, but by sharing her path.

So she starts small: offering advice to a few women at her local gym, sharing what's worked, listening, and encouraging. In the process, she reconnects with her own "Why."

Jasmine isn't chasing more. She's chasing *meaning*. Her strength now isn't just in her body—it's in her mindset. She's not afraid to evolve, shift, and lead. Her story reminds us that thriving in midlife isn't about holding on to what was—it's about leaning into what's next, with purpose.

WHICH ONE ARE YOU?

Maybe you saw yourself in Emma—ready to start, but unsure how. Or in Lisa—always beginning again, searching for something that sticks. Or in Jasmine—strong and steady, but craving new purpose.

No matter where you are, one thing's clear: they didn't wait for the perfect moment. They just took the next step. And you can, too.

You've already done something powerful—you paused to reflect. You got honest about what's working and what's not. Now it's time to move forward.

This is where insight turns into action. And the SPARK Framework gives you the tools to do just that.

You don't need a total overhaul. You need a path that fits *your* life—simple, doable, and designed to keep you moving forward, one step at a time.

CHAPTER 7

PLANNING THE PATH

E ver set a goal, feel super motivated, and then boom, life happens? You get busy, something throws you off track, and suddenly that plan you were so excited about feels impossible. Sound familiar?

Planning your path isn't about having it all figured out. It's about creating something that supports you as life unfolds.

The SPARK Framework gives you the tools to do just that, to map out your next steps with intention, stay grounded when life gets messy, and move forward at a pace that feels right for you.

Because let's be real: life *will* get in the way. Work deadlines, family obligations, unexpected stress, it's all going to happen. But when you're adaptable, you don't have to keep starting over every time things get messy. Instead, you adjust, shift gears, and keep moving forward.

This step is about preparing to succeed by setting boundaries, protecting your time and energy, and staying focused on what actually matters, without getting derailed by distractions or the need to do everything perfectly.

It's not just about finding time or choosing the right routine. It's about uncovering the habits, patterns, and mental blocks that keep pulling you off track. That's where your power is.

When you can recognize what throws you off and prepare for it, you're no longer reacting but instead you're planning with intention. You're making space for what matters and creating something that fits your real life.

This next part is all about laying that foundation. You'll get clear on what's been holding you back, learn how to protect your time and energy, and create a flexible path forward, one that supports your goals without demanding perfection.

You don't need a flawless plan. You need a flexible one that works *for you*.

IDENTIFYING TRIGGERS AND MENTAL BLOCKS

I had spent years teaching Pilates under someone else's rules, following their structure, their way of doing things. But I wanted more. I wanted the freedom to create a space where I could teach in a way that truly served my clients.

So I made the decision to go out on my own.

I started by meeting with a realtor, hoping to find a commercial space to open my studio. I came in prepared, full of ideas and excitement. But before I could even finish explaining what I was looking for, he dismissed me completely. No advice, no encouragement, no loan suggestions, just a quick brush off.

It was discouraging. For a moment, I wondered if maybe I wasn't ready. If maybe this dream was too big.

But deep down, I knew that moment wasn't really about the realtor. It was about the mental blocks I was still carrying—the quiet doubts that said, "You can't do this."

And I wasn't ready to listen to them anymore.

At the same time, my husband and I were looking for a new house—one that, ideally, had space for a studio. I hadn't given up on the dream. I was just trying to find a different way to make it happen.

Meanwhile, I had also lined up a teaching opportunity at someone else's studio. It wasn't ideal, but it felt like a step forward. I trusted the owner, and based on our agreement, I invested over $6,000 in new Pilates equipment to use in her space.

Then I got blindsided.

Another instructor went behind my back and told the owner she wanted the full Monday through Friday schedule. I was suddenly left with just Saturdays and Sundays, as if she were doing me a favor.

I sat in my car, stunned. I had already bought the equipment. I was ready to work. Now, it felt like everything was slipping through my fingers before I'd even gotten started.

Then my phone rang. It was the studio owner, Dr. Justine Bernard. "I'm honoring our agreement," she said. "You invested in this. You're going to teach here."

That moment meant everything. I felt seen. Respected. Reassured that I hadn't made a mistake.

I was starting to find my rhythm again, teaching at the new studio and feeling a bit more like myself. At the same time, my husband and I had been looking for a house—specifically one with space where I could eventually build something of my own. After weeks of searching and coming up short, we found it. A house with a garage already set up for a potential fitness studio. My husband looked around, smiled, and said, "That's the one." He believed in me, even before I fully believed in myself and that made all the difference.

Looking back, every setback, the dismissal from the realtor, the studio drama, the detours, helped me uncover the beliefs that were holding me back. They forced me to get clear on what I wanted, what I deserved, and how I was going to claim it.

I didn't need a perfect plan. I needed to trust myself enough to keep going.

Every time something doesn't go the way you planned, it's not a sign to quit, it's a chance to check in with yourself. Are you letting outside voices or past doubts make decisions for you? Or are you choosing to keep going, even when the path isn't clear?

You don't need a perfect setup. You don't need permission. You just need to believe that your vision matters, and be willing to take the next step, even when it's uncomfortable.

Because sometimes, the detour leads exactly to where you're meant to be.

WHY TRACKING PROGRESS KEEPS YOU GOING

When you hit a setback, it's easy to feel like you are starting over. But the truth is, you are not. You have already taken steps. You have already moved forward. The challenge now is recognizing that progress, especially when doubt starts whispering that you have not done enough.

That's why tracking your progress matters.

When we rely on memory alone, we tend to focus on what's left to do instead of how far we've come. But when you have something tangible, a journal entry, a checklist, a note on your phone, you have proof. Proof that you took that first step. Proof that you pushed through an obstacle. Proof that even when it felt like nothing was changing, you were still moving forward.

I've had many moments of self-doubt, thinking, *Who am I to do this when so many others seem more qualified?* Then I go back and look at an old email I sent, a class I taught, a challenge I pushed through. And suddenly, I remember that I did take action. I did find another way forward.

Tracking your progress isn't about patting yourself on the back. It's about keeping yourself grounded in reality when doubt tries to distort it. It's about seeing the evidence that you are growing, learning, and moving toward what you want.

So before you convince yourself you're stuck, take a moment. Look back at what you've already done. Write it down. See it in front of you. Because even on the days it doesn't feel like it, you are making progress.

Struggle to find time for workouts, meal prep, or self-care? The Midlife Time Management Planner (QR code) will help you prioritize what matters most.

ACCOUNTABILITY AND SUPPORT

One of the people who had the biggest impact on my fitness career was Dr. Justine Bernard, the owner of the studio I moved into. Justine is a master trainer in the Gyrotonic® Method and a doctor of physical therapy. She built a space that wasn't just about movement—it was about growth. Walking into her studio, you could feel it. No drama. No competition. Just support, community, and a shared passion for helping people feel better in their bodies.

She became more than just a colleague. She was a mentor. Over the years, Justine sent clients my way, offered guidance when I needed it, and created an environment where instructors could thrive. For a while, it felt like I had found the perfect place to teach.

But even in that supportive space, something inside me began to shift. It wasn't about the studio. It wasn't about Justine. It was about me.

I had this growing pull to create something of my own. I wanted to teach in a way that reflected my personal vision, to combine movement, mindset, and nutrition in a space that felt fully aligned with who I was becoming. And as hard as it was to imagine stepping away from something good, I knew deep down that it was time.

That's the thing about growth. It doesn't always come from discomfort. Sometimes, it comes from the quiet knowing that you're ready for more.

Justine never held me back. In fact, she showed me what true mentorship looks like. Support without strings. Guidance without control. She taught me that at some point, you stop waiting for someone to tell you you're ready, and you decide that for yourself.

If you've ever had someone believe in you like that, you know how powerful it can be. But the real shift comes when you start believing in yourself.

So I ask you. Who are your Justines? Who has been there when things got messy? And more importantly, are you letting their support push you forward, or are you using it as a reason to stay where you are?

Support matters. But so does self-trust.

This chapter of my story started with a setback, and it ended with a decision. I could keep playing small, or I could claim what I really wanted. And the minute I chose to trust myself, everything changed.

You don't need to wait for permission. You just need to take the next step.

FLEXIBILITY AND ADAPTABILITY

If at first you don't succeed, pour yourself a big glass of wine (or tea, whatever's right for you) and sit with it for a moment. Let yourself feel frustrated, disappointed, even a little sorry for yourself. That's human. But then, get back on the horse. Ask yourself, *What else can I do? Because this is not where I want to be.* Be willing to shift gears. A setback does not mean failure, it just means you are heading in a different direction. And whatever you do, don't feel guilty for changing course.

Emily had to learn this lesson the hard way.

Living by a strict plan, every day was mapped out, her career on a five-year timeline, her workouts the same every week. The routine gave her a sense of control, like she had everything handled. But when she tore her ACL during a ski trip, everything unraveled.

"I don't know what to do," she admitted in one of our sessions. "I feel like I'm losing all my progress. If I can't train the way I used to, what's the point?"

Her frustration was real. She had spent years building strength, showing up day after day. Now, forced to slow down, she felt helpless. But what she didn't realize yet was that this wasn't the end, it was an opportunity to learn a different way forward.

We shifted her focus from what she **couldn't** do to what she **could**. (Sound familiar? This mindset shift is crucial!) Instead of her usual high-intensity workouts, we worked on controlled strength movements, core stability, and

Pilates-based rehab. It wasn't what she had planned, but it was exactly what she needed.

At first, she resisted. It didn't feel like "real" training. But as the weeks passed, she saw something she hadn't expected, she was getting stronger in a new way. The injury had forced her to adapt, and in doing so, she discovered a side of fitness she hadn't explored before.

Months later, when she returned to skiing, she felt more stable than ever. Not because she had stuck to her original plan, but because she had been willing to pivot when life forced her to.

How often do we cling to rigid expectations, believing that if things don't go exactly as planned, we've somehow failed? Life rarely unfolds in a straight line. Flexibility doesn't mean giving up—it means adjusting, adapting, and staying open to new possibilities.

If you've been resisting change, consider this: *What if the detour is actually part of the path? What if the shift you didn't plan is the very thing that moves you forward?* Adaptability is not a weakness. It is one of your greatest strengths and it clears the way for something even more important: learning to reframe the thoughts that try to hold you back.

REFRAMING NEGATIVE THOUGHTS

One of the biggest mindset shifts you can make is learning to recognize negativity, whether it's coming from your own thoughts or the people around you. If you can't see how these messages shape your actions, it's easy to stay stuck without even realizing it.

I always thought I was good at filtering out negativity. I tried to avoid it whenever I could, and I made sure to teach my daughter, Melanie, to do the same. But when she was just eight years old, she turned that lesson back on me in a way I wasn't expecting.

PURSUE YOUR SPARK

At the time, we had a friend, Martina, who often invited us over for dinner. I appreciated it, especially during a time when money was tight as a single mom. Eventually, things got better, and I didn't need that kind of support anymore, but out of habit, we kept going over for dinners.

One night, as we were driving home, Melanie shifted in her seat and looked at me. "Mom, why are we still hanging out with her?"

I glanced at her in the rearview mirror, confused. "What do you mean?"

"She's the most negative person on the planet," she said, matter-of-factly. "She complains about her husband, her son, her life and you just sit there and take it."

Her words hit me like a slap. She was right.

My fingers tightened around the steering wheel, my mind replaying our last visit. Martina sat across the table, a glass of wine in hand, rattling off the same grievances as always. The resentment toward her husband. The constant frustration with her son. The never-ending list of things that made her unhappy. And I had sat there nodding, listening, absorbing it all.

After my divorce, most of my old friends had sided with my ex-husband. I had clung to the few connections I had left, maybe longer than I should have. And somewhere along the way, I stopped questioning whether that friendship was actually good for me.

That night, I couldn't stop thinking about what Melanie had said. How long had I been letting someone else's negativity seep into my life? And what else had I accepted as normal just because it was familiar?

Little by little, I pulled back. Not in a dramatic way, just enough to create some space. Life got busy, and our visits became less frequent. And while we're still in touch here and there, it's different now. That chapter has naturally closed, and I've moved on, carrying the good memories with me while also recognizing that I've outgrown that space.

Looking back, I realize how easy it is to stay in a dynamic that no longer serves you, whether it's a friendship, a job, or even your own negative self-talk. Sometimes, we don't even recognize we're stuck until someone else points it out.

So ask yourself:

> **"** *Have I ever stayed in a situation just because it was familiar?*
> *How did it feel to finally let go?*
> *Is there someone in my life right now whose negativity is*
> *weighing you down?* **"**

The thoughts we hold onto shape how we show up in the world. The stories we repeat become the limits we believe. But what if, instead of judging those thoughts, you started getting curious about them? What if you paused to notice what's been keeping you stuck, not to criticize yourself, but to meet it with understanding?

That's where self-compassion begins. Not with fixing, but with noticing. Not with doing more, but with being kinder to yourself as you grow.

SELF-COMPASSION AND PATIENCE

Guilt has a way of creeping in, making us question our choices and hold ourselves to impossible standards. I still catch myself second-guessing decisions I made years ago, wondering if I did the right thing. But I made the best decision I could with what I knew at the time. That's all any of us can do and it deserves compassion, not judgment.

A lot of the guilt we carry isn't even ours. It's passed down through generations of women expected to be perfect caregivers, mothers, and daughters. We're taught to feel guilty for saying no, for putting ourselves first, even for something as simple as taking an hour to ourselves. But those expectations aren't truth. They're just old stories we've inherited.

This is where patience becomes part of the practice. You can't undo a lifetime of guilt in a single day. It's a process. And every time guilt creeps in, the most powerful thing you can do is pause and ask: *Is this really mine? Or did I pick it up along the way?* That pause? That's self-compassion. It's giving yourself space to respond with care instead of pressure.

One of the hardest decisions I ever made was leaving my marriage.

When I think back to the early days with Ken, I remember how natural it felt to be together. We built a good life, had a rhythm, and for a long time, it worked. But over the years, something shifted. There were no dramatic fights or betrayals, just a growing realization that we wanted different things. The age difference between us of seventeen years, which once did not matter, started to feel like a widening gap. I was craving something more, not a different partner, but the freedom to make choices for myself.

I could have stayed. I would have been fine. But I did not want fine.

I remember the moment I knew. I walked into Ken's office, and before I even thought about it, the words came out. "We are all packed for tomorrow, we will leave for the airport at three o'clock. And besides, I want a divorce."

He stared at me. "What?"

"Yeah," I said. "I want a divorce. I don't like my life."

And that was it. No long debates, no drawn-out planning. I had spent years trying to convince myself to stay, but in that moment, I finally admitted the truth.

We tried counseling after I returned from the trip, but it only confirmed what I already knew. I sat across from the therapist and said, I do not love him anymore. I do not want this life. I will not doubt my decision.

The therapist nodded. Well, if you feel that way, there is nothing I can do for you.

That was the final confirmation. I was not looking for a way to fix it. I was ready to move on.

That did not mean it was easy.

For years, guilt lingered in the back of my mind. Not because I thought I had made the wrong decision, but because society teaches us that choosing ourselves is selfish. I had a good marriage and a stable life. Why wasn't that enough?

But guilt does not mean you made the wrong choice. It just means you are breaking a pattern.

Over time, Ken and I worked through the hard parts. We co-parented, became friends, and eventually, he and my now-husband Jan became close. The tension faded. The guilt softened. Life moved forward, just as it always does.

Self-compassion reminded me that it was okay to want something more. But it was patience that helped me stay with the discomfort of change while I figured out what that "more" could look like.

Letting go of guilt, choosing yourself, honoring what you need, these aren't things that happen all at once. They happen slowly, through small shifts and quiet decisions.

That's the power of patience. It makes space for something new to take root.

Now that you've given yourself the grace to reflect... Let's look ahead. Let's talk about what's next, and begin imagining the version of you who's already living it.

PURSUE YOUR SPARK

VISUALIZATION AND FUTURE-BASED THINKING

Where do you want to go? How do you want to feel in your body? What do you see for your career, your relationships, and your life ahead?

Visualization isn't just setting goals. It's creating a vision that excites and motivates you, one that feels possible and realistic for the person you are becoming.

I think about Brenda, a client who came to me feeling stuck. She had always been active but lately found herself exhausted, dealing with joint pain, and wondering if this was just how life was going to be from now on. During one of our first sessions, she sighed and said, "I just don't feel like me anymore."

She had tried different programs before, but when life got busy or she did not see immediate progress, she gave up. This time, she wanted something different. She wanted something sustainable, but more than that, she wanted hope.

So I asked her, "What do you actually want for yourself, not just now, but five, ten years from now?"

She hesitated at first, then her face softened. "I want to travel without worrying if my knees will hold up. I want to get on the floor with my grandkids and not struggle to get back up. I want to wake up in the morning and not feel stiff before my feet even hit the floor."

That was her vision. Not a number on the scale. Not fitting into old clothes. But a future where she felt strong, independent, and capable.

Once she could see that version of herself, everything changed. When she did not feel like working out, she reminded herself that movement was not about today. It was about her future self, the one who could walk all day on vacation without pain and wake up feeling energized instead of achy.

That vision kept her moving forward, even on the days when progress felt slow.

Now, take a moment to visualize your future…

> *How do you want to feel in your body five, or ten years from now?*
> *What do you want to be able to do?*
> *How can you start making choices today*
> *that align with that vision?*

Your future is not something that just happens. It is something you create with the actions you take now. Every time you move, nourish your body, or make a choice that supports your well-being, you are shaping that future version of yourself.

You do not need all the answers right now. You just need to start moving in the right direction.

ALL YOU'VE GOT IS ALL YOU NEED.

TAKING ACTION:
TIME TO PUT YOUR PLAN IN MOTION

You've taken the time to reflect, to assess where you are, and to get honest about what's holding you back. Now it's time to move forward, not with a massive overhaul, but with a clear, simple plan you can actually stick with. This is how you begin to build real momentum.

STEP 1: NAME WHAT'S HOLDING YOU BACK

Take a moment to ask yourself:
What's been getting in the way lately?
Is it time? Motivation? Doubt? A tendency to overthink?

You don't need to solve it all—just name it. That awareness is the first step toward shifting it.

STEP 2: CHOOSE ONE FOCUS AREA

Pick one thing to work on right now—just one.
Is it:

- **Mindset:** shifting a negative thought or setting a daily intention?
- **Fitness:** a short daily walk or committing to three workouts this week?
- **Nutrition:** prepping one healthy meal or staying hydrated?

Start small. Make it something you know you can follow through on.

STEP 3: LET SOMEONE IN

Who's in your corner? Think of one person who can support you—whether it's a friend, a coach, or someone on the same journey.

Let them know what you're working on. You don't need a cheer squad, just someone who sees you and keeps you grounded.

STEP 4: KEEP TRACK IN A WAY THAT FEELS NATURAL

Tracking your progress doesn't need to be perfect. It just needs to be consistent.

You could:
- Mark a calendar
- Use a habit tracker
- Write one sentence in a journal
- Or simply ask, "Did I show up for myself today?"

Find what feels right for you and stick with it.

STEP 5: STAY FLEXIBLE

Life will interrupt your plans. That's not failure—it's reality.

When that happens, ask:
What's one small way I can still show up for myself today?

Maybe it's a walk instead of a full workout.
Maybe it's a nourishing snack instead of the full meal you had planned.

Flexibility is what keeps you moving, not perfection.

This isn't about doing it all. It's about doing one thing—and doing it consistently.

Your plan doesn't need to be perfect. It just needs to be yours.

Now, let's check in with Emma, Lisa, and Jasmine to see how their plans are unfolding and how you might take your next step too.

CASE STUDIES

CASE STUDY #1: EMMA, 52

Balancing work, family, and finally putting herself on the list

When Emma finished her self-assessment, one thing was clear: she was ready to feel better, but had no idea where to start. Structured fitness? Nutrition plans? That was all new territory. She'd spent years caring for everyone else and putting her needs on the back burner. But not anymore.

Instead of trying to change everything overnight, Emma committed to just beginning. She chose a doable starting point: a 20-minute walk, five days a week. Nothing complicated, no pressure to "work out"—just time to move, clear her head, and reconnect with her body.

Food was next. She'd fallen into the habit of grabbing whatever was fast and easy, especially on busy workdays. But now, she started preparing just one home-cooked, balanced meal a day. Lean protein, veggies, whole grains—simple, satisfying, and doable. And when her energy dipped mid-afternoon, she swapped chips for fruit or a handful of almonds. Not because she had to, but because she wanted to feel better.

To keep herself accountable without feeling overwhelmed, she began journaling what she ate and how she felt, not to obsess but to learn. Over time, she saw what worked: skipping meals left her drained, while regular snacks and hydration kept her steady. Her awareness grew, and with it, her confidence.

On weekends, she tried something new: beginner Pilates. It initially felt awkward, but she laughed, followed along, and surprised herself by enjoying it. It wasn't about being good at it but about showing up for herself in a new way.

Emma's progress didn't come from willpower or discipline. It came from building small wins that fit into her real life. Every step she took reminded her: she didn't need a total transformation. She just needed a path she could walk—one she chose for herself.

CASE STUDY #2: LISA, 48

Health-savvy, but stuck in the start-stop cycle

Lisa didn't need a beginner's guide. She already knew how to eat well and move her body—she'd done it before. There were seasons when she felt strong, energized, and on top of it all. But staying consistent? That's where things kept falling apart.

After walking through her self-assessment, she finally saw the pattern: she wasn't failing, she was cycling. Start strong, lose momentum, feel guilty, stop, repeat.

So this time, she approached things differently. There were no extremes, no 30-day challenges, just small, sustainable changes she could actually keep up with.

She got back to what she loved: Cycling. Twice a week, she clipped in and rode with zero pressure to hit numbers, just to feel the wind and clear her head. On her busier days, she fit in shorter at-home workouts, some Pilates, a few bodyweight circuits—just enough to keep her rhythm going.

She let go of the idea that meal prep had to be perfect. Instead of cooking every meal in a batch for the week (and then feeling like a failure when she didn't), Lisa started prepping twice a week, keeping things flexible and simple. And when life got chaotic, she leaned into healthy convenience options without guilt.

What really changed for Lisa, though, was her mindset. One off day used to feel like she had to start over. Now? She just reset. A quick walk, a balanced meal, and even a few minutes of journaling reminded her that progress wasn't about perfection—it was about coming back, again and again.

Lisa's story isn't about doing more. It's about doing what works and letting that be enough. With fewer rules and more flexibility, she's finally building something that lasts.

CASE STUDY #3: JASMINE, 61

Strong, seasoned, and stepping into her next chapter

Jasmine has always pushed herself. She's trained for marathons, competed in fitness events, and built a lifestyle that's as disciplined as it is inspiring. Fitness and nutrition aren't new to her; they're part of her identity. But after taking stock in her self-assessment, she realized something: she's not done growing. She's just getting started—again.

This next phase isn't about achieving more. It's about refining, fine-tuning, and evolving with purpose.

Her training still challenges her, but now she's tuning into the most important details—recovery, mobility, and longevity. She's incorporating deeper stretching routines, prioritizing sleep, and experimenting with tools like deep tissue massage and mindfulness practices. It's not about doing more—it's about training smarter.

She started exploring new movement styles to keep her workouts fresh and exciting. A Pilates class here, a yoga session there— nothing drastic, just new ways to keep her body engaged and her mind curious. That variety helps her avoid burnout and connects her to the joy of movement.

Even with years of solid nutrition habits, Jasmine's now experimenting with timing and balance, adjusting her macros to fuel her performance and recovery more precisely. She's not overhauling her diet—she's fine-tuning it, staying curious about how her body responds to small changes.

But the most meaningful shift? Jasmine feels called to give back. Whether mentoring women at her gym or casually encouraging friends on their health journeys, she realizes that her story has power and is ready to share it. She's no longer just the student. She's stepping into the role of mentor, guide, and example.

Jasmine's story reminds us that thriving doesn't mean standing still. It means evolving, staying open, and leading with intention. Her next chapter isn't about proving anything—it's about living fully and showing others what's possible.

This book isn't about becoming someone else; it's about becoming *more* of who you already are.

Whether you're starting like Emma, trying to stay consistent like Lisa, or fine-tuning what already works like Jasmine, your journey is yours. You don't need to be perfect. You don't need to have it all figured out. You just need to take the next right step.

Because growth doesn't come from changing who you are. It comes from embracing yourself—fully—and choosing small, meaningful shifts that help you feel stronger, healthier, and more *you* every day.

You're not behind. You're not broken. You're just getting started.

YOU'VE ALREADY STARTED. NOW KEEP GOING.

You've chosen your first step. You've seen how midlife women like Emma, Lisa, and Jasmine are putting their plans into motion, just like you.

You don't need to wait for the perfect time or the perfect plan.
You've already begun.

Now it's about **keeping that momentum going**, through the messy days, the moments of doubt, and the unexpected curveballs.

Reflection prompt:
What's one thing I've done this week that moved me forward, even a little?

Next up, we'll shift from reflection to action, so you can take the first real steps toward your goals and build the kind of momentum that lasts.

CHAPTER 8

ACTION TOWARD GOALS

I didn't exactly choose fitness, fitness sort of found me.

A friend practically dragged me to my first class at the YMCA, convinced I needed to do something just for myself. And honestly? She wasn't wrong.

At the time, I was feeling completely disconnected from my body. Not long before, I had worked for the German Foreign Service, confident, independent, and in great shape. I felt strong in who I was and the life I was building.

Then everything changed. I became a mom, which I loved. But along with that came a body I barely recognized. During my first pregnancy, I gained fifty pounds. And the baby was only nine pounds, so...

I felt stuck. Frustrated. Overwhelmed. I didn't even know where to begin.

Maybe you've been there too, wanting to take action, but unsure of how to start or if the effort is even worth it.

Here's what I've learned:

You don't need a perfect plan to begin. You just need to show up.

So I went to that YMCA dancersize class, even though I didn't feel ready, even though I was uncomfortable, even though I was tired. It wasn't glamorous. It wasn't some magical transformation. But it was something. It was movement. It was a "yes" to myself. It was the beginning of momentum.

That's how change really starts, not with motivation, but with one small decision to move forward.

That first class turned into two. Then into a routine. I started to reconnect with my body. I began to feel stronger, not just physically, but mentally too. My confidence slowly returned, and I remembered what it felt like to feel like *me* again.

Taking action means starting where you are and building momentum through small, consistent steps. It means using the resources you have, not waiting for the stars to align. It means embracing challenges with an open mind and a determined heart. Saying "yes" to opportunities, even when they seem daunting they create momentum. And yes, it can be scary. But showing up despite the fear is how we grow.

WHAT ABOUT YOU?

If you're feeling stuck, ask yourself:

> *What's one small action I can take today without overthinking it?*
> *Am I letting perfectionism hold me back from simply beginning?*
> *What's a movement or activity I might actually enjoy? (It doesn't have to be the gym!)*
> *What would it feel like to start focusing on strength, energy, and confidence instead of just numbers on a scale?*

Taking action doesn't have to be overwhelming. It can be as simple as moving for 10 minutes, trying a new class, or even just committing to show up, for yourself, your goals, and your future.

You're not just planning anymore—you're making it happen. One small step at a time.

Let's go.

Because once you take that first step, the next one gets easier.

Momentum builds confidence. And confidence? Changes everything.

To become a better instructor and lead stronger, more engaging classes, I signed up for a teacher training program. I'd already mentioned earlier that when the trainer asked if I wanted to teach, I said yes—though honestly, I was mortified. Me? Teaching a room full of people, bouncing around to music? It felt wild.

But I practiced nonstop, determined to prove I could do it. I studied the routines, rehearsed the moves over and over. The training focused on dance aerobics—Zumba-style choreography where you had to learn sequences *and* teach them back to a group.

Then came test day. I thought I had it nailed.

I didn't.

"You're not teaching to the beat of the music," the instructor told me.

I thought, *What? Of course, I am!*

"What do you hear?" she asked.

"Singing."

She shook her head. "You're teaching to the lyrics. You need to teach to the beat."

I still didn't get it. Then she walked over, grabbed my hand, and placed it on the speaker. "Feel that?" she said.

And suddenly, I did.

That moment changed everything. I wasn't just hearing the music—I was *feeling* it. But just understanding the beat wasn't enough. I had to completely retrain myself to teach from the ground up. Before every class, I put my hand on the speaker, rooted myself in the rhythm, and drilled it until it became second nature.

There was something nobody knew, and I never thought much of it. But failing that test? That was a big deal to me.

I am deaf in one ear and have been for as long as I can remember. Most of the time, it wasn't an issue. But that day, I realized how much it had shaped the way I learned movement and how I had to adapt in ways I never considered before.

It made me think about how I process rhythm, especially as someone who dances Argentine tango. Tango isn't just about following music, it's about feeling your partner's movements, sensing the connection, and adapting in the moment. Maybe that's why placing my hand on the speaker was the missing link.

A month later, I tested again. I passed.

It wasn't about passing a test. It was about learning to listen—to movement, to my students, and to what the body truly needs.

That failure turned out to be one of my best teachers.

WHAT THIS STORY TEACHES US

At the time, I didn't think of it as courage. I wasn't standing there feeling brave or bold.

Honestly? I felt nervous, uncertain, and totally out of my element. But I still said yes.

Looking back, that's *exactly* what courage looks like.

It's not a loud, fearless roar—it's the quiet choice to try something that feels unfamiliar.

To say yes when your brain says, "This is wild, what am I even doing?" To sign up, show up, practice, and keep going—even after failing the test.

That's the real lesson here.

This story is about resilience. About adapting when things don't go as planned. About learning to trust the process when the path forward isn't clear.

So now I'll ask you:

> **"** *Have you ever said yes to something that scared you?*
> *Have you had a moment where things didn't go as planned*
> *and you had to find a new way forward?*
> *Can you remind yourself to trust the process, even when it feels shaky?* **"**

WHAT DOES COURAGE LOOK LIKE?

Courage doesn't always feel courageous. It often feels awkward, uncomfortable, and unsure.

But that's the moment you grow.

Most people come to me for Pilates. But what if Pilates is not your thing? That is okay. Strength training, resistance bands, or even small shifts in your nutrition can make a difference. The key is choosing something and committing to it.

And commitment takes courage. It is easy to try something once and quit. But real growth happens when you push past the initial awkward phase, the part where it feels unfamiliar, uncomfortable, or even a little discouraging. That's why I always encourage my clients to commit to their choice and stick with it for at least six weeks. Give yourself enough time to see if it is working before deciding it is not for you. If after six weeks it still does not feel right, we adjust. But you have to give yourself that chance first.

But courage in midlife is about more than just starting a new workout. It is about choosing yourself, even when it feels uncomfortable. It is about starting before you feel ready. It is about letting go of who you used to be and embracing who you are now.

It takes courage to say, "I matter, too" when you have spent years prioritizing everyone else. It takes courage to try something new when you are afraid you might fail. And it takes courage to stop chasing the past version of yourself and start creating a future where you feel strong, capable, and energized.

I see this kind of quiet courage in midlife women all the time. They're still scared. Still feel guilty for putting themselves first. But something shifts when they start asking, "Why not me?" They watch other women take bold steps and begin to believe they can, too.

Courage isn't about having it all figured out. It's about showing up anyway— taking one step, then the next, and realizing along the way that you're stronger than you thought.

Ask yourself:

> *Where in your life are you holding back
> because you feel you are not ready?
> When was the last time you put yourself first without guilt?
> What would happen if you allowed yourself to take up space?*

Your future is not something that just happens. It is something you create. And when you have the courage to start, you will always find a way forward.

COURAGE ISN'T ABOUT BEING FEARLESS—IT'S ABOUT MOVING FORWARD DESPITE THE FEAR.

EMBRACING VULNERABILITY

Asking for help takes courage. The first step to asking for help is admitting you need it. That's not always easy. It takes courage to say, "I want to change something, and I need support to do it." But that moment of honesty is where real growth starts.

For many women, vulnerability feels uncomfortable. It's easier to say, "I'll figure it out myself," than to admit, "I don't have all the answers."

We've been conditioned to believe independence equals strength. That pushing through alone somehow makes us more capable. But that mindset? It's what keeps us stuck.

Strength is not about pretending to have everything under control. It's about being real with yourself. Instead of thinking, "I should be able to do this on my own", or "Needing help means I'm failing."

What if you shifted that thought to: "I am learning, and it's okay to ask for support"?

Tanja's Turning Point.
She was the one everyone leaned on, the caretaker, the dependable one who never asked for help. But when it came to her own health, she felt stuck. Exhausted. She kept saying, "I just need more willpower, more discipline, more time."

When we first spoke, she told me, "I feel like I should be able to figure this out on my own. It's just working out and eating better... right?" But deep down, she knew it was more than that.

The real shift came when she stopped trying to white-knuckle her way through it and let herself be supported. She started showing up—for her workouts, her meals, and herself. And instead of seeing support as weakness, she saw it as strength.

Today, she's not just stronger in her body, she's stronger in her boundaries, her confidence, and her ability to say, "This matters. I matter."

The Truth About Strength. So many women believe they're supposed to handle everything.

But the strongest people aren't the ones who push through in silence. They're the ones who know when to reach out, when to lean in, and when to say, "I can't do this alone and that's okay."

What Vulnerability Really Means. Vulnerability is admitting you don't have all the answers.

It's the moment where growth begins, whether in fitness, nutrition, or life itself. It's being seen. It's accepting help without guilt. It's not a weakness. It's human. It's letting go of perfection and embracing progress instead.

Ask yourself:

> **"**
> *Thinking back, where in your life*
> *have you avoided asking for help?*
> *What held you back? Was it fear, pride, or the belief that you*
> *should be able to do it all?*
> *What changed when you finally let someone in?* **"**

VULNERABILITY IS NOT WEAKNESS. IT'S A DOORWAY.

It allows for support, connection, and the kind of transformation that only happens when you stop trying to figure it all out alone.

EMBRACING DISCOMFORT: THE KEY TO GROWTH

You have already done one of the hardest things, admitting you want change. You're letting go of the idea that you need to do it all alone. But now comes the next step.

Change is uncomfortable. Growth doesn't happen in your comfort zone. It is easy to stay where things feel safe and familiar, but that is not where real progress is made.

Many people have ingrained "shoulds" that hold them back. They tell themselves, "I should be further along. I should be able to do this on my own. I should be as fit as she is." But who decided these "shoulds" for you? Where did they come from? More importantly, do they actually serve you?

The Trap of the Shoulds

I tell my clients this all the time: The only thing you "should" be is happy. And they usually nod, maybe half-agree. Because moving through life without some kind of expectation feels unnatural. "Should" feels like a driving force, a motivator. But more often than not, it picks at your brain in a bad way, making you feel like you are always falling short.

If I had only focused on where I "should" be, what others told me I needed, the equipment I should have, the studio I should run, I wouldn't be where I am today.

Like training for a 5K. You set your goal, and ideally, you want to run the whole thing. But what if you can't? What if you need to walk part of it? Does that mean you failed? No. You still covered the distance. You still got stronger. You still learned about your body. And at the end of it, you are going to feel way more empowered than if you had never tried at all.

And here's what most people miss: reaching a goal isn't the end. You don't finish the race and go back to the couch. Because the real win isn't the finish line. It's who you become in the process—stronger, more energized, more *you*.

And here is another truth. Your journey is yours. It is not your sister's, your best friend's, or your neighbor's. It won't look like theirs, and it is not supposed to. Comparison will only pull you away from what actually matters and what works for you.

Let Go of the Rules That Don't Serve You

Take a moment to reflect:

> *Where are the "shoulds" in your life holding you back?*
> *What would happen if you let go of them?*
> *How would your progress look different if you focused on what*
> *feels right for you instead of what is expected?*

Growth is not about waiting for the perfect moment or the perfect plan. It is about showing up, even when it is uncomfortable.

The Power of Habits: Make Progress Feel Effortless

Discomfort is part of growth, but growth isn't about pushing yourself in big ways. It's about the small choices you make every single day.

Most women don't struggle because they lack motivation. They struggle because they rely on motivation. They feel inspired, they take action, but life gets in the way. A bad night's sleep, a stressful day, or a busy schedule throws everything off. Before they know it, they're right back where they started, wondering why they can't stay consistent.

The real key to lasting progress is not willpower or motivation. It's habits.

Women who succeed in the long run don't wake up every morning debating whether or not they will take care of themselves. They don't rely on feeling motivated. They have built habits that make their success automatic.

Think about brushing your teeth. You don't question whether or not you will do it. You just do it. Now imagine if your workouts, nutrition choices, and self-care felt just as natural.

That is where habit stacking comes in.

The Habit Stacking Strategy: Make It Easy to Stay Consistent

Habit stacking is one of the simplest ways to build a new habit without feeling overwhelmed. Instead of trying to "find time" for something new, you attach it to something you're already doing.

Here's how it works:

You take an existing habit you already do every day, like making your morning coffee, brushing your teeth, or checking your emails and pair it with a small new habit that supports your goal. The key is to keep it simple. So small, in fact, that it feels almost impossible to fail.

What if you used that familiar habit as a trigger for a small, meaningful change?

For example, if you already drink coffee every morning, add a new habit onto that routine by drinking a glass of water first. If brushing your teeth is something you never skip, you can use it as a cue to do five squats afterward. If checking emails is part of your workday, you can stack a habit of standing up and stretching right before opening your inbox.

The reason this works is because you're not forcing yourself to create a habit from scratch. Instead, you're using an existing habit as a natural trigger, which helps the new behavior stick without requiring extra effort or willpower.

> *What's one habit you already do every day that could help you build momentum toward your goal?*

Over time, these small habits become automatic. The more you stack, the easier it becomes. Now that you know how to stack habits into your daily routine, the next step is making sure they actually stick. And that starts with one simple rule: start small.

Make It Stick: Small, Consistent Wins

The biggest mistake people make with habit-building is starting too big. They try to go from zero to one hundred overnight, hour-long workouts, cutting out entire food groups, committing to massive changes. It's too much, too fast, and leads to burnout.

Instead, start ridiculously small. Tiny habits, done consistently over time, create big results.

If you want to start strength training, do one push-up today. Just one. If you're trying to get more steps in, walk for two minutes.If you want to meditate, close your eyes and breathe deeply for ten seconds.

Sounds almost too easy, right? That's the point. When something feels easy, you'll actually do it. And once it becomes automatic, you can build on it.

Take Hani, for example. She wanted to start working out again, but every time she planned a full 45-minute routine, life got in the way, work, kids, unexpected errands. So we came up with something simple: every morning after brushing her teeth, she'd do five lunges. Just five.

At first, it felt almost silly. But she stuck with it. A few weeks later, those five lunges turned into ten. Then she added a few wall push-ups. Eventually, she was doing a 15-minute bodyweight routine most mornings, without needing motivation, because it had become part of her rhythm.

Hani didn't overhaul her life overnight.

She made it stick, one small win at a time.

The goal isn't perfection. The goal is to make showing up feel effortless.

Tracking small wins keeps you motivated. Use the Workout Progress Tracker (QR code) to log your workouts and see your strength build over time.

CHALLENGING THE BOUNDARIES WE SET FOR OURSELVES

We all set limits on what we think we can do, usually without realizing it. Whether believing we're too old to try a new move, thinking we can't lift heavier weights, or falling into habits without questioning them, these limits are usually more mental than physical.

Debbie came to me for Pilates because she wanted to get in shape. She was committed, showing up every week, practicing at home, and getting stronger. But we never really talked about nutrition. She was putting in the effort, and I could see the changes in her body.

Then one day, in the middle of class, she looked at me and said, "I just realized something. Every night, I sit down with my husband, and we eat M&Ms while watching TV. I don't even want them. I just eat them because they're there. Why am I doing this?"

That small realization changed everything. Once she saw what was happening, she did not have to force herself to stop. She simply *chose* to stop. Not because she felt restricted, not because she was following a diet, but because she no longer felt like she had to. Within a year, she lost 20 pounds. Not by overhauling her life. Not by cutting out foods she loved. Everything shifted for Debbie the moment she made one intentional decision to prioritize herself.

Awareness was the first win. Once Debbie saw how one unconscious habit was sabotaging her progress, she could finally take control and move forward.

So many of the limits we put on ourselves are not really limits at all. They are just thoughts we have repeated so many times that we accept them as truth.

> **"**
> *Where in your life are you following a habit without questioning it?*
> *What is something you have convinced yourself you can't do, but have never actually tried?*
> *Are you holding yourself back because of a real challenge, or just because it feels unfamiliar?* **"**

We all have these moments. Maybe you've always believed you're not strong enough to lift weights. Or that Pilates isn't for you because you're not flexible. Or that changing your eating habits is too hard. What if you tested that belief? What if you did the thing you have been avoiding, just once?

You don't have to overhaul your life overnight. You don't have to be perfect. But when you start questioning these invisible boundaries, you don't just change a habit, you change the way you see yourself. And that's when real transformation begins.

STAYING FLEXIBLE: THE KEY TO GROWTH

The key to growth is flexibility, not just in movement, but in the boundaries and goals we set for ourselves.

We create boundaries to protect our energy, health, and time. They help us stay focused, maintain balance, and avoid burnout. But sometimes, without realizing it, those same boundaries start to hold us back. Instead of keeping us safe, they keep us stuck.

Take a moment to check in: *Are your boundaries still serving you, or are they subtly standing in your way?*

One of the biggest mistakes we make is letting others define our limits. Just because a friend is training for a 5K doesn't mean you have to. Just because someone else is changing their diet doesn't mean their approach is right for you. Boundaries are personal. They are meant to serve you, not shape you into someone else's version of success.

And, boundaries aren't set in stone.

Boundaries can and should evolve as needed. There's a difference between respecting a real limitation and holding yourself back out of habit or fear. What once may have been a necessary boundary might no longer fit the person you're becoming. Maybe you told yourself you could never lift weights, but now you are curious about getting stronger. Maybe you believed you weren't disciplined enough to stick with a workout routine, but now you realize you just needed something you actually enjoy. Maybe you've convinced yourself that change is too hard, but deep down, you know you're ready.

Here's something to think about:

 Are the boundaries in your life empowering you, or quietly boxing you in?
Are they rooted in your own truth, or were they shaped by what others expect from you?
And what if... one of those limits you've held onto no longer fits who you are becoming?

So the real question becomes: ***Are the limits you've set still aligned with who you are, or are they based on who you used to be?***

Jackie's the kind of client who likes structure. She thrives on plans, lists, and checking off every box. When she committed to strength training, she followed her program to the letter, never missing a workout, hitting her macros perfectly, and staying on track. She loved the sense of control, the feeling that if she just did everything right, the results would follow.

Then, as it does, life happened. A stressful work project threw off her schedule. She missed one workout, then another. A weekend trip made meal prepping impossible. By the time Monday rolled around, she felt like she had already failed.

"I messed up," she told me, frustration all over her face. "I was doing so well, and now I've lost my progress. I feel like I'm starting over."

I could hear the disappointment in her voice, the way she had convinced herself that missing a few workouts meant undoing everything. But the truth was, her progress hadn't disappeared. Her strength was still there. Her habits had not vanished. The only thing that had changed was her mindset.

"What would you say to a friend who was in your position?" I asked.

She paused, then sighed. "I'd tell them to just pick up where they left off."

Exactly.

That was Jackie's breakthrough moment. She realized she did not have to be perfect. She did not have to restart just because she missed a few steps. Instead of quitting, she adjusted. She swapped an hour-long session for a quick 20-minute workout. She focused on getting back into her routine instead of punishing herself for stepping away.

And once she stopped chasing perfection, she became more consistent than ever.

We have all heard that it takes six weeks to build a habit, but that is not the whole story. Six weeks is just a starting point, not a finish line. Some habits stick right away, others evolve. The key is not quitting when things feel off, but instead figuring out what needs to shift.

So ask yourself:

> *Where in your life are you stuck on the idea that something has to be "all or nothing"?*
> *What is one small adjustment you could make instead of quitting altogether?*
> *How would your progress look if you gave yourself permission to adapt rather than expect perfection?*

Growth is not about rigid rules. It is about staying committed to the process. Keep going, keep learning, and trust that small steps add up.

TAKING ACTION: YOUR NEXT STEPS

Taking action isn't about having a perfect plan. It's about noticing what gets in the way and learning how to move through it. This part of the journey is where you build resilience, not by avoiding challenges, but by learning how to work with them.

Let's simplify the process so it feels less overwhelming and more doable.

STEP 1: START WHERE IT MATTERS MOST

You don't need another perfect plan. You need to know where to begin.

Before jumping into a new routine, take a breath.

Ask yourself: "What part of my life actually needs the most care right now?"

Maybe your workouts are consistent, but you feel like your nutrition is all over the place. Or maybe it's your mindset, you're constantly battling your inner critic. Instead of trying to fix everything, pick one area that feels most important or doable right now. That's your starting point. That's where the shift begins.

Reflection: *What's one area I feel called to focus on right now? What's one small action I can take this week to support it?*

STEP 2: START WITH ONE SMALL ACTION STEP

Once you've chosen your focus, break it down into manageable steps. Big change doesn't happen all at once; it starts with one clear, intentional step.

If your focus is mindset, you might work on catching and reframing one negative thought. If it's fitness, maybe it's one 10-minute walk this week. If it's nutrition, plan one simple, balanced meal you actually enjoy.

Small steps that feel doable are more powerful than big plans that never leave your head.

Reflection: *What small step will I take this week?*

STEP 3: CHALLENGE THE "SHOULDS"

We all carry around ideas of what we think we "should" be doing. But where do those expectations come from and do they actually help?

Maybe you've always told yourself, "I should work out five days a week," but life doesn't allow for that right now. Instead of constantly feeling like you're falling short, give yourself permission to adjust.

Try this: "I will move my body in a way that supports my life and energy right now."

Releasing the pressure of unrealistic "shoulds" frees you up to move forward in a way that feels good.

Reflection: *What's one 'should' I can release, and what belief will I replace it with?*

STEP 4: CREATE SUPPORT THAT FEELS GOOD

You don't have to rely on motivation or willpower alone. Having someone, or something, to help you stay on track makes all the difference.

This could be a quick weekly check-in with a friend, a simple reminder on your phone, or a sticky note reminding you why you started. Support doesn't have to be big or formal; it just needs to be consistent and kind.

Reflection: *How will I hold myself accountable in a way that feels supportive, not stressful?*

STEP 5: NOTICE REAL PROGRESS

Progress isn't just measured by the numbers. It's how you feel. How you show up. How you respond to the tough days.

Did you pause before reacting? Make a better food choice? Choose rest instead of pushing through?

These are the wins that matter. Start noticing them. Start celebrating them. They prove you're growing, even when it doesn't feel big.

Reflection: *What's one small win I had this week that I might've overlooked?*

STEP 6: ADJUST INSTEAD OF GIVING UP

Setbacks will happen. Plans will fall apart. That's normal. The real progress comes from how you respond.

Instead of quitting, ask: *What needs to shift?*

Maybe your morning workouts don't work anymore, so you try lunchtime walks. Maybe your meal plan feels too rigid, so you simplify it. Adjusting doesn't mean you're giving up. It means you're being smart and staying in motion.

Reflection: *What's one thing I can adjust this week to keep moving forward?*

You don't need to be perfect. You just need to keep showing up and trust that each small step is getting you closer to the life you want.

Instead of quitting, adjust.

Because sometimes it's not your effort that's the problem, it's the story you're telling yourself about what should be happening by now. This is where mindset comes in.

Before you can build lasting habits or make real change, you have to face what's happening between your ears. The doubt. The perfectionism. The comparison. The belief that you're "just not the kind of person who…"

Let's go there next.

CHAPTER 9

MINDSET OBSTACLES

W e constantly run into obstacles while pursuing the things we care about. Some are external barriers, like financial struggles or lack of support. Others are internal battles, like self-doubt and comparison. I've faced both throughout my journey.

When I first had the idea for Pilates with Resist-A-Ball, I wasn't a well-known instructor. I was a beginner teacher, still learning, still finding my place. The more I worked with clients, the more I experimented with ways to make Pilates more engaging. One day, I grabbed a stability ball and started incorporating it into traditional Pilates mat exercises. The result was immediate. My clients loved it. They felt more supported in some movements and more challenged in others. The ball helped them connect to their bodies in a new way.

I was excited. I could see the potential. But almost as quickly as the excitement came, so did the doubt. This isn't real Pilates. Pilates should only be done on a mat or reformer. No one will take this seriously.

I tried to push the thoughts away, but they lingered. The Pilates world was rooted in tradition, and what I was doing didn't follow the rules. Who was I to introduce something new? I wasn't a master teacher. I didn't have decades of experience. Maybe I was getting ahead of myself.

But every time I worked with my clients, I saw the results. They were improving. They were excited. They kept coming back, asking for more. That was real. So I kept going. I refined the exercises, tested different approaches, and built the program step by step.

At first, some dismissed it. But over time, the skepticism faded. More people became curious. They saw how it worked and how it helped people move better. Eventually, what started as an experiment became a full training method. I just refused to stop following my curiosity.

Looking back, I realize that the biggest obstacle wasn't the industry's doubt. It was my own. Obstacles don't mean stop. They mean rethink, refine, and push forward in a new way. Some roadblocks will force you to find a different path. Others will challenge you to shift your mindset. Either way, obstacles aren't meant to stop you. They're meant to shape you.

Let's unpack some key concepts that will help you identify and navigate the obstacles in your journey.

THE POWER OF RECOVERY

I used to think taking a break meant falling behind. That if I wasn't constantly moving forward, I was losing momentum. But I've learned something important: a pause isn't failure — it's part of the process.

Recovery doesn't mean stepping away from your goals. It means rebuilding the strength to keep going. When we hit obstacles, our instinct is to push harder. To grind. To force progress. But growth often happens in the stillness, when we stop, breathe, and reassess. Without recovery, we don't gain momentum, we lose ourselves.

Judy learned this the hard way. Running was her escape, her therapy, her way of proving she was strong. She loved the rhythmic pounding of her feet against the pavement, the burn in her legs, and the rush of endorphins after a long run. But she ignored the warning signs: tightness in her calves, aching knees, the dull pain in her hip that lingered longer each time. She convinced herself that pushing through meant progress.

Until the day her body stopped her for good.

She was midway through a run when a sharp pain shot through her knee, stopping her in her tracks. She tried to shake it off, stretch it out, walk it off. But this time, there was no pushing through. No finishing the run. Just the crushing realization that she had done too much.

Frustration filled the following weeks. Sitting still felt unbearable. She watched others run, feeling like she was falling behind. She tried to convince herself that if she could get back out there, everything would be fine. But deep down, she knew. Her body wasn't the enemy. She had been fighting against it instead of working with it.

So, for the first time, she did something different. She rested. She stretched. She listened. And when she finally returned to running, something had changed. She wasn't healed; she felt stronger, lighter, and more in control. She had learned that real strength isn't about how far you can push; it's about knowing when to pull back.

Recovery isn't wasted time. It's the space where you rebuild. It's where your body heals, your mind clears, and your energy returns. It's what allows you to come back stronger instead of dragging yourself through the next challenge on empty.

We often think progress means constantly moving forward, but real growth can happen in the pause when we stop with intention to regain the strength, clarity, and focus we need to keep going.

So, if you're facing an obstacle and feel stuck, ask yourself:

> *Do I need to push forward,*
> *or do I need to step back and recharge?*
> *Am I permitting myself to rest without guilt?*
> *How can I use this time to come back stronger?*

Judy thought that slowing down meant losing progress, but recovery was what made her stronger. She learned that listening to her body didn't mean giving up; it meant setting herself up for success. What if your next breakthrough isn't when you push harder? What if it is when you step back, recharge, and come back stronger?

Real growth doesn't just come from effort. It comes from rest, repair, and resilience.

MENTAL ROADBLOCKS: RESET, REFOCUS, RE-VISUALIZE

We all hit mental roadblocks. Those invisible barriers that make us doubt ourselves, second-guess our abilities, or feel like we're spinning in place. Sometimes, they show up as self-doubt ("I'll never be able to do that"), other times as procrastination ("I'll start next week"), and sometimes as frustration ("Nothing I do is working").

But remember, a roadblock isn't the end. It's just a moment to pause, reassess, and figure out the next move.

My client, Sarah, recently landed a big promotion, a career-changing opportunity that she'd worked hard for. But with it came longer hours, endless meetings, and a schedule that left little room for anything else. She's constantly exhausted, overwhelmed, and ready to quit the program she had already invested in.

"I just don't have time," she told me, rubbing her temples. "There's no way I can keep up with everything."

I could hear the frustration in her voice, the weight of responsibilities piling up. She wasn't giving up because she didn't care. She was drowning in expectations, and something had to give. But instead of letting her walk away, I asked her one simple question. "What if you didn't have to do it all? What if you just did something?"

At first, she hesitated. "Like what?"

"Like one ten-minute workout. Or choosing one mindful meal. Just one small action each week."

She sighed, unsure. But she agreed to try.

Week by week, she kept going. A short stretch before bed. A mindful breakfast instead of skipping. A quick walk between meetings. And slowly, something shifted. She didn't just stay in the program. She felt stronger. She started feeling in control again. She realized that progress wasn't about doing everything perfectly. It was about showing up in the small moments, taking action where she could, and proving to herself that she could make it work.

Real growth doesn't come from all-or-nothing thinking. It comes from consistency, even when life feels chaotic. Think about a time you felt stuck. Maybe you wanted to start working out, but a little voice in your head said:

"You're not in shape enough to do this." "You'll never stick with it, so why even try?" "You should be further along by now."

Those thoughts are the real roadblock, not your ability, not your schedule, not even the challenge itself. The biggest obstacle is usually the belief that you can't succeed and it's all too much.

Before you assume you're stuck, take a step back. Is the challenge in front of you real, or is it the fear of stepping outside your comfort zone? Are you resisting because it's impossible or because it feels hard?

Sometimes, the answer is persistence: giving yourself time and patience to keep going. Other times, it's about shifting gears, looking at the situation differently, or allowing yourself to adjust without guilt.

A roadblock only stops you if you let it. If you start seeing obstacles as moments to pause and reassess instead of reasons to quit, you'll realize you're not stuck. You're just figuring out your next step.

ALL-OR-NOTHING THINKING

Could it be possible that in-between is good enough? Sometimes, we get so caught up in all-or-nothing thinking that we can't move forward. I've been there. I've always wanted it all, but at some point, I had to ask myself: How much am I actually willing to do? And if I'm not willing to push to the extreme, do I really want it? Or is in-between good enough?

For me, this question hit hard when it came to running. One day, I was clocking 60-mile weeks, pushing my limits, feeling invincible. The next, I was sidelined: knees screaming, body breaking down, my entire routine coming to a screeching halt. It wasn't just an injury. It was a wake-up call.

I remember sitting on my porch, icing my knees, watching other runners go by, and feeling this deep frustration. Running had been my identity, my thing. If I couldn't do it at full intensity, was I even a runner anymore? Was there a point in doing it at all?

For weeks, I wrestled with this. Part of me wanted to push through, to prove I could get back to where I was. But another part of me started asking different questions. Did I actually love running, or had I just been chasing bigger numbers? Was I willing to destroy my body just to say I hit 100 miles a week? Or was there a way to still enjoy running without breaking myself in the process?

That was the moment I questioned it all: What if *showing up imperfectly* was still showing up? What if running could be more about joy than proving something?

Maybe you've felt this, too. Maybe you've told yourself, "If I can't do it perfectly, why bother?" But what if success isn't about doing the most, but about doing what *actually* works for you?

Ask yourself:

> **"** *Are you pushing for more because it truly serves you or because*
> *you think you should?*
> *Is the way you're chasing your goals sustainable,*
> *or is it wearing you down?*
> *What would happen if you let go of extremes and focused on*
> *what actually feels good and supports*
> *your long-term well-being?* **"**

Because real success isn't about doing everything at the highest level. It's about finding a way to keep going without burning yourself out in the process. In-between isn't settling. It's what makes progress sustainable.

FEAR OF FAILURE KEEPS YOU STUCK

Fear of failure is something we all wrestle with. That little voice that says, *If I don't reach my goal, I've failed.* I see it all the time with my clients, especially when it comes to nutrition.

Patti was one of them. She came to me frustrated, convinced she would never get her eating habits under control. "I always mess it up," she sighed.

"I do great for a few days, and then the second I eat something 'bad,' I figure I've blown it, so I might as well just start over next week."

She was stuck in that all-or-nothing thinking. Either she ate perfectly, or she felt like a failure. One "wrong" meal, one moment of stress eating, and she was convinced she had ruined everything. So, instead of adjusting, she'd give up entirely, only to repeat the same cycle again.

FAILURE ISN'T PERSONAL, IT'S DATA

I asked her, "What if one meal doesn't define you? What if instead of starting over, you just kept going?"

At first, she didn't believe it could be that simple. But we started small. Instead of labeling foods as "good" or "bad," we focused on balance. If she had a heavier meal, she'd follow it up with something nourishing instead of spiraling into guilt. If she indulged in dessert, she'd enjoy it and move on. No more starting over. No more throwing away progress over one decision.

She stopped obsessing over being "perfect" and started making choices that actually worked for her life. She realized that progress wasn't about never slipping up; it was about learning to keep going even when things weren't ideal.

That's the thing about failure. It's not personal. It's just *data*. A moment that gives you feedback on what's working and what isn't. When Patti started looking at her habits that way, she stopped seeing a bad meal as proof she wasn't capable. Instead, she started wondering, *What can I learn from this?*

AVOIDANCE IS THE REAL FAILURE

Fear of failure doesn't just make us doubt ourselves, it can keep us from starting altogether. I've worked with women who stayed stuck not because they weren't capable, but because they were scared of getting it wrong. But here's what I've learned: staying exactly where you are out of fear? That's what keeps the cycle going.

Patti almost walked away because she thought anything less than perfect wasn't worth doing. But when she dropped that pressure, she found something that *actually* worked, and she's still going strong.

PROGRESS ISN'T LINEAR, SETBACKS ARE PART OF SUCCESS

Another thing we forget all the time is that progress isn't linear. You won't always move in a straight line. You rarely will. There will be weeks when you feel unstoppable and weeks when you feel like you've lost momentum. That's normal. Just because you hit a rough patch doesn't mean you're back at square one. The people who succeed aren't the ones who never struggle. They're the ones who learn to *recover* from struggle and learn from it.

So take a moment and think about this:

> **"** *Has fear of failure ever held you back, not because you couldn't
> do something, but because you were afraid
> you wouldn't get it just right?
> What if you shifted your focus from trying to be
> perfect to just being consistent?
> What if you measured your progress not by flawless execution,
> but by the fact that you kept going, even when it got messy?* **"**

Reaching your goal might take time. You might take detours. But that doesn't mean you've failed. Sometimes, the bravest thing you can do is to try again, with a little more grace, a little less pressure, and the trust that every small step forward still counts.

HEIKE YATES

"YES, AND" INSTEAD OF "BUT"

We all have moments where we talk ourselves out of taking action. We say things like:"I don't have time." "I don't feel like it." "Why should I?" "I tried that already." "I'm not good enough."

These thoughts create roadblocks, shutting down possibilities before they even start. They keep us stuck, convincing us that if something isn't easy, it isn't worth doing.

My client, Melissa, struggled with this. She wanted to get back into a fitness routine but kept talking herself out of it. "I'd love to start working out, but my schedule is too hectic…I want to be healthier, but I always fall off track." She truly *wanted* change, yet every time she considered taking action, she followed it with a reason why she couldn't.

So I challenged her. "What if, instead of saying but, you said yes, and?"

She gave me a skeptical look. "What do you mean?"

I explained. "Instead of stopping yourself with a but, acknowledge the challenge and find a way forward."

She thought for a moment. Then she tried it.

"I'd love to start working out…yes, and I know my schedule is tight, so I'll start with just ten minutes a day."

"I want to eat healthier…yes, and I know meal prepping feels overwhelming, so I'll focus on making one better choice at a time."

See the difference? Instead of letting obstacles stop her, she accepted them, adjusted, and moved forward anyway.

THE POWER OF SHIFTING YOUR MINDSET

Obstacles are a part of life. The key isn't to avoid them but to think outside the box, stay flexible, and keep taking steps forward. The "Yes, and" mindset helps you move from excuses to solutions instead of shutting yourself down. Embrace progress over perfection, knowing that even small actions count. It keeps you adaptable when things don't go as planned, so you don't quit altogether.

It's a small shift with a big impact. Instead of feeling powerless against your challenges, you take ownership of what you can do, even if it's not perfect.

Next time you catch yourself saying *but*, try replacing it with *yes, and*. Notice how it shifts your perspective and opens up new possibilities.

Ask yourself:

> *What challenges have I been avoiding because I keep saying but?*
> *How can I reframe it with "yes, and" to take action?*
> *What's one small step I can take today to*
> *move forward despite the obstacle?*

Because success isn't about avoiding obstacles. It's about meeting them head-on, adapting, and moving forward, one *yes, and* at a time.

EMBRACE IMPERFECTION

Most women walk into my Pilates studio with hesitation. They're already worried about doing something wrong before they've even begun. They hold themselves to impossibly high expectations, feeling like they should be doing more, should have it all figured out, and should get it perfect on the first try.

But here's the thing. Perfection isn't the goal. Progress is.

When you move, it's not about following a rigid plan. It's about tuning in to what your body needs, adjusting in the moment, and trusting that small changes lead to big results. That's why I don't structure sessions in advance. Instead, I ask, "How was your day? Where is your stress? Where is your mind at?" Because what works one day might not be right the next.

And here's something to remember: changing course doesn't mean you've failed. It means you're paying attention. If something isn't working, you pivot. You try something else. You learn what feels good, what challenges you, and what helps you grow. That's not failure. That's awareness.

So what if you stopped expecting perfection from yourself? What if you permitted yourself to be *in progress instead*?

You don't have to get everything right the first time. You just have to show up, stay open, and keep going. The moment you stop demanding perfection is the moment you start making real progress.

"   *What If Imperfection Was the Goal?*   **"**

Joseph Pilates once said, *"We are striving for the ideal and not for perfection, because the ideal is different for everybody."*

So, what if, instead of fearing imperfection, we embraced it?

"   *What if trying and adjusting was the whole point?*
What if mistakes weren't setbacks but stepping stones?
What if success wasn't about getting it right but about showing up for yourself, even when it feels messy?   **"**

Many of my clients begin to see movement differently: not as something to perfect but as something to experience, learn from, and grow through. They realize that progress doesn't come from getting everything right. It comes from showing up, staying consistent, and becoming more aware of what their bodies need.

And the best part? When one woman takes that first step, others follow. They see her letting go of perfection, embracing the process, and they start to think, *Why not me?*

It's not about having it all figured out. It's about giving yourself the chance to take that first step—messy, imperfect, and completely yours.

SHIFTING YOUR PERSPECTIVE

Recognizing obstacles isn't just about seeing what's in your way, it's about understanding how your mindset shapes your response to them. Whether it's comparison, fear of failure, all-or-nothing thinking, or perfectionism, these mental roadblocks can make challenges feel bigger than they really are.

But what if, instead of letting these obstacles stop you, you saw them as opportunities to adjust and grow?

Take a few minutes to reflect:

" *How often do I compare myself to others, and how does it impact my motivation?*
What past successes can I remind myself of when I start doubting my abilities?
Do I believe I deserve success, and if not, why?
How can I start building self-worth and confidence through small, consistent actions? **"**

These aren't just reflection questions. They are tools to help shift your mindset, reshape your habits, and take control of your progress. Because mindset obstacles will always show up. The difference between staying stuck and moving forward is how you respond to them.

Challenges don't just show up in our thoughts. They show up in our bodies, too. Just as comparison, fear, or perfectionism can hold you back mentally, injuries, time constraints, and fitness setbacks can create roadblocks in movement. But the approach is the same. Progress isn't about perfection. It's about flexibility, self-awareness, and a willingness to adapt.

Because whether the obstacle is in your mind or your body, the solution is always the same, keep going.

TAKING ACTION: OVERCOMING MINDSET OBSTACLES

Sometimes the biggest roadblocks aren't external, they're the thoughts that keep you stuck. Self-doubt. Comparison. The pressure to do it all perfectly. These mindset obstacles can hold you back before you even begin.

But mindset can shift. And that shift starts with awareness and small, supportive actions.

STEP 1: NOTICE THE THOUGHT THAT HOLDS YOU BACK

Start by paying attention to what you're telling yourself.

It might sound like: *"I always fall off track."* Or *"I'm too far behind to start."*

These thoughts feel true, but they're just stories. Stories you can rewrite.

Try asking: *What thought is keeping me stuck and what else might be true instead?*

STEP 2: REFRAME IT

Once you notice the thought, flip it. Not into fake positivity, but into something honest and supportive.

"I always fall off track" becomes "I can always return and keep going."

"I should be doing more" becomes "I'm doing what works for me at a pace I can maintain."

When your thoughts shift, your energy shifts. And so does your progress.

STEP 3: REINFORCE IT WITH ACTION

Now take one step that supports your new mindset. It doesn't need to be big. Just something that says: *I believe in this new story.*

Maybe it's going for a walk because you said you would. Maybe it's prepping one meal. Maybe it's speaking to yourself with kindness today.

Your mindset changes when your actions match your intention.

Reflection Prompt: What thought am I choosing today and what small action will I take to support it?

Using the Accountability Tracker (QR code), you can track your progress and check in with your mindset. Let it be a reminder that your mindset is a muscle, and every step you take strengthens it.

CHAPTER 10

FITNESS OBSTACLES

A melia had been training with me, growing stronger and more confident with every session. She was ready to take the next step and wanted to add a day or two at the gym on her own.

At first, she was excited. She had a plan, she felt motivated, and she was determined to push herself. But the moment she stepped into the weight room, doubt crept in. The space was packed with heavy lifters, the sound of plates clanging and machines whirring. She looked around at people moving confidently through their workouts and felt completely out of place.

"What if I'm doing it wrong? What if people stare? What if I don't belong here?"

She hovered near the treadmills, telling herself she would lift weights next time. But week after week, she kept avoiding it. She stuck to what was familiar, even though she knew she wanted to push herself further.

One day, she finally admitted her frustration. "I want to go in there, but I just freeze. I don't know what to do, and I don't want to look clueless."

I could hear the disappointment in her voice. She wasn't lacking motivation. She lacked a clear plan.

We didn't do anything fancy. No intense circuits. No trying to master five machines in one day. I showed her how to start with just three simple exercises using free weights. We practiced until the movements felt familiar. She started to carry herself a little taller. I could see the shift happening.

And then came the moment that really mattered: The next time she walked into the gym, she did it on her own. No second-guessing. No scanning the room for approval. She picked up the weights, did her routine, and walked out with that quiet kind of pride that comes from showing up for yourself.

That's what progress really looks like. Not perfect. Just possible.

That's what letting go of perfection can look like. Not flashy. Not dramatic. Just steady, doable, and real.

Physical obstacles, whether it's time, injuries, or simply not knowing where to start, can feel just as overwhelming as the mental roadblocks that keep us stuck. But there is always a way forward. Don't let these challenges stop you. It's about breaking them down, finding solutions, and adjusting as needed. No single approach works for everyone, so the key is creating a plan that fits you.

Up next, we will explore some of the most common fitness obstacles and excuses. But we'll unpack them so you'll know how to navigate them and keep moving, no matter what's in your way.

"I DON'T HAVE TIME"

Time feels like the biggest obstacle to a lot of people. We fill our days with endless to-dos, work, and responsibilities, leaving little room for ourselves.

But when we look closer, it's not about having time. It's about how we *prioritize* it.

There's always something demanding attention. Work deadlines, family obligations, unexpected tasks. It's easy to push movement to the bottom of the list, convincing ourselves that we'll start when things slow down. But does that time ever come? Or does life keep moving, filling every available space?

We often think of exercise as something extra, something separate from daily life. But what if it was just part of it? What if movement wasn't something you had to find time for but something that fit into the time you already have?

Instead of saying, "I don't have time," ask yourself, "Where am I placing myself on my list of priorities?"

"I'M NOT SEEING RESULTS"

Frustration can set in quickly when results aren't showing up as fast as we'd like. It's easy to feel like all the effort isn't paying off or like nothing is changing. But fitness is a long game, not a sprint. Real, lasting change takes time.

My client, Laura, felt this firsthand. She had been showing up consistently, doing her workouts, eating well, and expecting to feel a major difference. At first, she had more energy, her body felt stronger, and she was excited about her progress. But after a few months, she hit a wall. She wasn't seeing the same changes anymore.

She sighed and looked away, frustration bubbling just under the surface.

"I'm doing everything I'm supposed to. So why does it feel like nothing's working anymore?"

She was ready to quit. But instead of giving up, I asked her to pause. "What's changed since you started?" I asked.

She thought about it. "I guess I don't wake up as stiff as I used to. I can get through a workout without feeling completely wiped. And...I don't feel as stressed after long workdays."

She was making progress. It only looked different from the way she had been measuring it. *Not all progress is visible.* More energy, better sleep, feeling stronger, and less stress are shifts that happen long before you notice external changes. But they matter just as much. Progress isn't just about what you see in the mirror. It's how you feel, how you move, and how your body supports you in daily life.

Plateaus are normal. The key is recognizing that they aren't a sign to stop, although they could be a sign to adjust. Growth isn't linear, and results don't always show up when we expect them to. But every effort counts, even when it doesn't feel like it.

What if, instead of focusing on what hasn't changed yet, you paid attention to what *has*? What if progress wasn't about a result but about how you keep showing up, no matter what?

"THIS WORKOUT IS SO BORING"

We've all been there, staring at the clock, counting down the minutes, wondering why time moves so slowly when we're doing a workout we don't enjoy. The excitement we once felt fades, and suddenly, fitness feels like a chore instead of something we look forward to.

Judy came into the session drained. Her energy was low, her body language even lower.

"I know this is good for me," she admitted, "but I'm just not feeling it."

It wasn't that she'd lost her motivation, it was that the routine had lost its spark.

When movement becomes monotonous, motivation naturally drops. It's not that you've lost the drive; it's that your brain craves variety, challenge, and a sense of progress. Doing the same thing over and over without change starts to feel like running on a hamster wheel, draining your energy instead of fueling it. Once I knew Judy was feeling this way, we completely changed her home workouts. Instead of focusing on Pilates, we shifted her routine to strength training. The change gave her something new to work toward, challenged her differently, and reignited her motivation.

Maybe your body is ready for something new. Maybe the challenge is gone, and your routine isn't pushing you in the same way anymore. Or maybe the missing piece isn't the workout itself but the *way* you approach it.

The key isn't pushing through something that feels like a drag. It's about noticing when your routine needs a refresh, something that helps you re-engage and feel excited about moving your body again. Movement isn't just meant to be endured. It can be something that energizes you, lifts your mood, and makes you feel *alive*.

"I DON'T KNOW WHAT I'M DOING"

Feeling intimidated by starting something new is completely normal. Whether it's stepping into a gym, trying a new workout, or joining an activity for the first time, that uncertainty can feel overwhelming. But the key is not to let it hold you back.

Olivia had always dreamed of hiking in Rocky Mountain National Park. She had seen the photos: jagged peaks, winding trails, and views that stretched for miles. But whenever she thought about actually doing it, doubt crept in.

"What if I can't keep up? What if I get too tired? What if I slow everyone down?"

So she kept putting it off. She told herself she needed to get in better shape first. She needed to train. She needed the right gear. She needed to feel *ready*. But, *ready* never came.

When she shared her hesitation with me, I suggested she start with something more approachable: the C&O Canal in Maryland. Although a flatter trail, it has beautiful scenery. It was the perfect way to build confidence before tackling the mountains.

The morning of her first hike, she felt nervous. At the trailhead, she hesitated, watching other hikers stride past her with ease.

"Maybe I should just go for a walk around my neighborhood instead."

But instead of turning back, she took the first step.

The first mile felt harder than she expected. The steady walking made her legs ache, and she had to stop more often than she wanted to catch her breath. She kept glancing over her shoulder, worried that people behind her were annoyed that she was moving too slowly.

But as she settled into the rhythm of the trail, something shifted. She didn't focus on how far she had left to go. Instead, she started focusing on what she was doing at that moment, moving forward, step by step.

By the time she finished, she felt something new: a sense of accomplishment. She wasn't worried about how fast she was going or whether she had done it *right*. She had begun. And that was enough.

The truth is, no one starts as an expert. The only way to get more comfortable is to keep showing up, learning, and giving yourself permission to be a beginner. If you don't know where to start, just start *somewhere*. It doesn't have to be perfect. It just has to be a step forward.

PURSUE YOUR SPARK

"I DON'T FEEL LIKE IT"

Let's be honest, there will be days when you just don't want to. Not because you're lazy. Not because you're doing something wrong. But because your brain is wired to resist change. It wants comfort. Familiarity. The couch.

But here's the part we often forget: you don't have to *feel like it* to follow through. You don't need motivation to take action. You need a decision.

So, let's simplify it.

Don't think about the whole workout. Just commit to five minutes. Put on your sneakers. Step outside. Start with a stretch. Breathe. Move. See what happens.

Because most of the time? The hardest part is just starting. And once you do, momentum kicks in. That five minutes turns into ten. You finish your walk, your workout, your session and you feel a little more like *you* again.

This is how you build consistency. Not with big, perfect days, but with small, ordinary ones done on purpose.

"I'M TOO OLD AND TOO BROKEN"

Maybe you've had an injury, arthritis, or chronic pain, and it feels like your body is working against you. Or maybe you're thinking, "I'm not as young as I used to be." It's easy to believe that getting older means slowing down. The truth is that movement is still for you. It may look different than it used to.

Danielle thought the same thing when she walked into her first session. She had knee pain, a stiff back, and a long list of reasons why she wasn't sure she could exercise anymore. "I don't want to hurt myself," she admitted. "And honestly, I don't even know where to start."

What got her to sign up for her first session wasn't motivation, it was a moment on the living room floor. She'd been playing with her grandkids, and when it came time to get up, she struggled. Her granddaughter looked at her and asked, "Grandma, do you need help?"

That moment hit her. She didn't want to sit out on the fun. She wanted to stay in the game. So instead of focusing on what she *couldn't* do, we focused on what she *could*. Gentle movements. Smart progressions. Exercises that made her feel strong and safe.

And just a few months later, Danielle wasn't just moving better, she was back on the floor playing, laughing, and getting up much easier.

Fear of injury is real, and so is the frustration of not moving like you once did. But that doesn't mean the movement is off-limits. The key is to focus on what feels good and supports your body instead of forcing exercises that break it down. Strength training, Pilates, and swimming are all great ways to build strength and mobility without extra strain.

You don't need to be 25 to get stronger and healthier. Midlife is about choosing exercises that support you, not break you down. Fitness isn't about competing with your younger self or anyone else. It's about becoming the strongest, healthiest version of you today, wherever you are.

As you move through your fitness journey, you might return to this list of obstacles, and that's okay. Roadblocks happen. But they're not reasons to stop. They're just moments that remind you to adapt, adjust, and keep going. No matter your age or past injuries, you're never too old and never too broken to start feeling better and stronger today.

FINDING YOUR WAY FORWARD

Obstacles always appear, but they don't have to stop you. Whether it's a busy schedule, low motivation, or feeling like your body isn't what it used to be, it is about finding ways to adapt instead of giving up.

Take a moment to reflect:

> **"** *What's the biggest fitness roadblock holding me back right now?*
> *Is this a real limitation, or is there another way to approach it?*
> *What's one small step I could take today to move past it?* **"**

When you shift the way you look at obstacles, they lose their power. A packed schedule doesn't mean you can't move; it means finding ways to sneak in movement where you can. Feeling unmotivated doesn't mean you skip movement altogether. It means starting small and seeing where it takes you. Progress isn't about waiting for the perfect moment. It's about choosing to move forward, even in small ways, right now. Every step counts, even the imperfect ones.

FITNESS OBSTACLES: FINDING WHAT WORKS FOR YOU

Fitness challenges don't always sound like "I don't want to move." More often, they show up as:

"I don't have time." "I'm not seeing results, so what's the point?" "I don't even know where to start."

But the solution isn't doing more, it's doing what fits your life.

STEP 1: NAME WHAT'S GETTING IN THE WAY

Is it time? Motivation? Confidence? Or just not knowing what to do?

Be honest with yourself and write it down. Naming it is the first step to moving through it.

STEP 2: RETHINK WHAT COUNTS

I used to think that if I couldn't do a full workout, it wasn't worth doing. But when I let go of the all-or-nothing mindset, everything changed.

Ten minutes. A walk around the block. Stretching before bed. It all counted.

So does yours.

STEP 3: TAKE ONE STEP THIS WEEK

If time is tight, schedule just ten minutes. That's it. Put it on your calendar and show up. If motivation is low, skip the stuff you dread. Dance in your kitchen, walk with a friend or do something that feels good. If you're unsure where to start, try something simple: a walk, bodyweight squats, or a short video from your workout library.

You don't need to do it perfectly. You need to move in a way that works for you.

Reflection Prompt: *What's my biggest fitness obstacle right now? What's one small action I can take this week to move through it?*

Movement is just one piece of the puzzle, though. What you eat fuels how you feel, how you recover, and how much energy you have to show up in your life. And just like movement, nutrition isn't about perfection. It's about finding what works for you and building sustainable, not restrictive habits.

Just like fitness challenges can make it hard to stay consistent, nutrition obstacles can feel just as frustrating. Maybe you struggle with meal planning, emotional eating, or figuring out what works for your body. Perhaps you start strong but fall off track when life gets busy.

Next, we'll discuss the most common nutrition obstacles and how to navigate them so you can fuel your body in a way that feels good, is realistic, and aligns with your goals.

CHAPTER 11

NUTRITION OBSTACLES

Nutrition advice is everywhere, and it's exhausting. One day, carbs are the enemy, and the next, they're essential. Some say fats will help you lose weight, while others warn against them. It's no wonder so many of us fall into the trap of fad diets, hoping for a quick fix.

I know because I lived it.

After my pregnancy, I gained 50 pounds, and for the first time in my life, I felt completely lost when it came to my body. Nothing fit the same. I avoided mirrors. I told myself I would get back in shape, but between sleepless nights, stress, and the overwhelming pressure of doing everything right, I didn't know where to start.

So I did what so many women do. I turned to diets.

Scarsdale, the cabbage soup diet, low-fat everything. I followed the rules, starved myself, and waited for the weight to disappear. And sometimes, it did for a little while. But it always came back. Every diet felt like a cycle of hope, struggle, and failure.

I remember one evening in particular. Standing in my kitchen, staring at yet another bowl of cabbage soup, stomach growling, I felt this sinking realization: *I can't live like this.* I was exhausted. I was miserable. And I had no idea what else to do.

That's when I started questioning everything I had been told about dieting. The more I learned, the more I saw the lies I had believed for so long. The lies about good and bad foods, about restriction being the only way to lose weight, about my worth being tied to a number on the scale.

I let go of the idea that eating had to be perfect and started focusing on what my body actually needed.

Everything changed, how I ate, how I moved, how I *felt* in my own skin. For the first time in years, I wasn't just following a plan, I was listening to *me*.

If you've ever felt overwhelmed by nutrition, you're not alone. Let's break down the biggest nutrition obstacles that might be holding you back and explore how to ditch the confusion for a healthier, more effortless relationship with food.

INCONSISTENT EATING HABITS

Life gets busy, and sticking to regular eating patterns can feel impossible. Skipping meals or grabbing quick snacks may seem convenient, but it often leaves you low on energy and frustrated with your progress.

Mia knew this cycle all too well. Mornings were always rushed, so she'd grab a coffee and head straight into her day. Lunch was unpredictable. Some days, she'd forget to eat until mid-afternoon, other days, she'd snack on whatever was nearby. By the time dinner rolled around, she was starving, reaching for anything quick and satisfying. She'd eat fast, often past the point of fullness, and then wonder why she felt sluggish and bloated afterward.

"I don't get it," she admitted. "I'm not eating that much, but I feel like I have no energy, and I'm not seeing the progress I want."

She wasn't eating too much. She wasn't eating enough *consistently*. Her body was constantly playing catch-up, leading to energy crashes, cravings, and a pattern of overeating later in the day.

Once Mia recognized the pattern, rushing through her days, skipping meals, and grabbing whatever was closest—she made a few small but powerful changes.

She started by tossing a handful of almonds and a piece of fruit into her bag every morning. That way, when she was stuck in traffic or dashing between appointments, she had something to keep her going instead of hitting the vending machine or powering through with nothing at all.

Instead of skipping lunch entirely (which she often did), she set a gentle reminder on her phone: *Take 10 minutes for you.* Sometimes that meant a full meal. Other times, just a hard-boiled egg and some veggies. But it was intentional. It was fuel.

She also began prepping a couple of simple meals on Sundays, nothing fancy, just things she could reheat and enjoy without effort. A batch of quinoa salad, some grilled chicken, or pre-washed greens ready for a quick throw-together bowl.

The game-changer wasn't eating at perfectly scheduled times. It was *noticing* when her body needed something and having what she needed ready. She stopped running on empty, and for the first time in a long time, she had steady energy to show up fully for her day.

SOCIAL TEMPTATIONS

Family gatherings, parties, and nights out can feel like a minefield of temptations. The dessert table calls your name, and someone insists, "Just have one more drink!" Saying no can feel uncomfortable. No one wants to seem rude or feel left out.

Isabella struggled with this every time she went out with friends. She wanted to make healthier choices, but the moment she sat down at a restaurant and saw everyone ordering cocktails and appetizers, her resolve faded. "I don't want to be the only one not indulging," she admitted. "And if I start, I find myself saying 'whatever' and just go all in."

One dinner in particular stuck with her. She planned to order something balanced, but once the breadbasket hit the table and drinks started flowing, she got caught up in the moment. By the end of the night, she felt uncomfortably full and frustrated with herself. "I wasn't even enjoying the food that much. I was just eating because everyone else was."

Truthfully, social settings don't have to derail your progress. The challenge isn't the food itself. It's the mindset around it. You don't owe anyone an explanation for what's on your plate or in your glass. Social events are about connection, not just food. When you give yourself permission to make choices that serve your health goals, you take the pressure off. Does that mean pacing yourself, setting boundaries, or enjoying a little without going overboard? You decide. Enjoy the moment, but on your terms.

FOOD CRAVINGS

We all have those moments when we crave something salty, sweet, or cheesy, and it feels impossible to resist. Cravings often strike when we're stressed, bored, or emotional, making it easy to reach for comfort foods instead of what our bodies actually need.

But cravings aren't random. There's a reason you might be reaching for chocolate at night or salty chips in the afternoon. Our bodies send signals based on what they need, and sometimes, cravings are our way of trying to fill a gap, whether it's physical, emotional, or simply out of habit.

Why do we crave sweets? Sugar cravings can stem from blood sugar fluctuations, lack of sleep, or even emotional comfort. If you're skipping meals or going too long without eating, your blood sugar can drop, triggering an intense desire for something sweet to give you quick energy. It's also common to crave sugar when you're tired because your body is looking for an easy fuel source.

Why do we crave salty foods? Craving salty snacks can sometimes mean you're dehydrated or low on certain minerals like sodium or potassium. Stress can also play a role. When cortisol levels rise, your body may crave salty, crunchy foods as a form of relief.

Why do we crave comfort foods like cheese or fried foods? Rich, fatty foods trigger the brain's reward center, releasing dopamine (the feel-good hormone). If you're craving creamy, cheesy, or fried foods, it might be a need for more healthy fats in your diet or the emotional association of comfort.

Cravings don't mean something is wrong. They just mean your body is asking for something, whether it's fuel, hydration, or relief from stress. The key is learning to decode the craving instead of automatically giving in. Before grabbing a snack, pause and check in. Are you truly hungry, or is this a craving? Try drinking water, waiting a few minutes, or doing something else to shift your focus. If you still want it, find a way to satisfy the craving in a balanced way, like swapping chips for crunchy nuts or opting for dark chocolate instead of a candy bar.

Cravings don't have to derail you. They just need a little awareness and a better plan.

HEALTHY EATING FEELS EXPENSIVE

Shopping for organic, whole foods can feel like it costs a fortune. It's easy to get discouraged when eating healthy seems out of budget, especially when trendy health products and specialty items are priced higher than their processed counterparts.

But here's the truth: you don't need to shop at premium stores or fill your pantry with expensive superfoods to nourish your body.

The real challenge isn't the price tag—it's the belief that eating well has to cost more. Yes, processed convenience foods are often cheaper upfront. But they're low in nutrients, leave you hungry faster, and don't provide the energy your body truly needs.

Whole foods like vegetables, fruits, grains, and proteins may seem pricier, but they offer long-lasting nourishment. They help you stay full longer, which means less mindless snacking and fewer "emergency" food runs.

The key? Making smart, sustainable choices. That means planning your meals ahead of time, buying only what you'll actually eat, and focusing on foods that give you the most value. Think eggs, canned beans, oats, frozen vegetables, leafy greens, and simple proteins like chicken or tofu. These everyday staples are affordable, filling, and give your body the energy it needs, without relying on expensive, trendy health products. For example, instead of pricey kale chips, grab a big bag of frozen spinach.

Skip the $9 protein bar and make a quick hard-boiled egg or snack on a handful of almonds. Swap that $8 green juice for a simple apple and a glass of water.

You don't need fancy ingredients to eat well. You just need a plan that works for you..

COMPLICATED MEAL PREP

If spending hours in the kitchen after a long day sounds exhausting, you're not alone. Between work, family, and everything else on your plate, cooking can feel like just another chore.

Ava felt this every night. She wanted to eat healthier and cook more at home, but by the time she finished work, the idea of chopping, cooking, and cleaning up felt overwhelming. Most nights, she'd settle for takeout or throw together something quick, even if it wasn't what her body really needed.

"I know I'm supposed to plan meals ahead," she told me, "but I just don't have time to cook everything for the whole week."

That's where her mindset needed a shift. She had assumed that meal prep meant spending hours in the kitchen cooking full meals in advance. But it doesn't have to look like that.

Instead of cooking everything ahead of time, Ava made a few smart tweaks to make her evenings easier. She started rinsing and chopping veggies while she brewed her morning tea. She grilled extra chicken one night to use in salads and wraps the next day. She kept staples like cooked rice, pre-washed greens, and hard-boiled eggs in the fridge. Nothing complicated, just small things that saved time when it mattered most.

It wasn't about being perfect. It was about having a few go-to ingredients ready so dinner didn't feel like a big project every night. A little bit of effort earlier made healthy eating feel doable—not like another task on her to-do list.

Meal prep doesn't have to be complicated. The Meal Prep Cheat Sheet (QR code) has simple steps to make it easier, and the 3-Day Meal Ideas will help you get started with no guesswork.

CONFLICTING INFORMATION

Keto, intermittent fasting, low carb, high protein. Everyone has a different opinion on what is healthy. No wonder it feels overwhelming to know which direction to go.

Becki felt like she had tried everything. She counted calories, cut carbs, tracked macros, and read every ingredient label, convinced that if she just found the right formula, everything would fall into place. She followed one plan after another, always hoping this time would be different. But no matter what she did, the results never lasted.

She was exhausted.

"I don't want to be on a diet," she told me, "but I want to lose the weight and keep it off."

Her days revolved around food rules. "Should I eat this? Should I avoid that? Am I getting enough protein? Am I eating too many carbs?" Every meal felt like a test she had to pass. And yet, after all that effort, she still wasn't where she wanted to be.

So instead of putting her on yet another restrictive plan, I helped her shift her focus. She did not need more rules. She needed a way of eating that fit her life, something she could actually maintain.

At first, it was uncomfortable. She was so used to tracking and overthinking her meals that letting go of the diet mindset felt like stepping into the unknown. But little by little, she started trusting herself again. She paid attention to how food made her feel instead of just looking at numbers. She focused on balance instead of perfection.

And the results followed.

She lost four pounds of body fat, built strength, and saw her yoga practice reach a whole new level. But more importantly, she stopped feeling like food was something to control. She was no longer stuck in the cycle of chasing the next perfect diet. Instead, she found a way of eating that gave her energy, fit her lifestyle, and felt sustainable. There is no single right way to eat. Diet culture promotes extremes. Instead of getting caught in that cycle, focus on what works for you. Your body, your lifestyle, your long-term goals. There is no one-size-fits-all approach. Use the tools in this book to find a way of eating that feels good and results that last.

EMOTIONAL EATING

Turning to food for comfort when you're stressed or overwhelmed is incredibly common. You are not alone. Food can bring a sense of relief, a moment of escape, or even a feeling of control when everything else feels chaotic. But when it becomes the main way to cope, it can lead to overeating, guilt, and frustration.

Evelyn knew this cycle all too well. After long, exhausting days, she would come home, drop her bag by the door, and head straight to the kitchen. Without thinking, she would open the pantry and grab a handful of crackers, then a few more. Before she even realized it, she had finished half the box.

She was not hungry. She was just *done with life.*

She had spent the entire day putting out fires at work, rushing from one thing to the next, and handling everyone else's needs. Food gave her something to do, a way to unwind.

At first, the familiar crunch and salty taste felt soothing. But as she sat on the couch, looking at the empty box beside her, the comfort faded. Instead, guilt crept in. "Why do I keep doing this?" she thought. "I tell myself I'll stop, but I always end up right back here."

She did not lack willpower. She responded to stress the way many people do. The brain craves comfort, and food is one of the fastest, most accessible ways to get it.

Instead of trying to eliminate emotional eating entirely, the goal is to add more ways to cope with what causes emotional eating in the first place. Evelyn started checking in with herself before reaching for food. Was she hungry, or was she just overwhelmed? Some nights, she still wanted the crackers, and that was okay. But she also started experimenting with other ways to unwind, like taking a short walk, stepping outside for fresh air, or stretching for a few minutes before eating. She still allowed herself to enjoy food, but she no longer relied on it as her only source of comfort.

Small shifts like these can make a big difference. Emotional eating is not about lack of control. It is about recognizing patterns and finding other ways to support yourself.

By checking in with yourself and identifying which of these obstacles might be holding you back, you are already taking the first step toward lasting change. Small adjustments, made consistently, can lead to big progress over time.

Not sure what a balanced portion looks like? The "How to Measure Portions" guide (QR code) offers an easy visual breakdown to help you stay on track without counting every bite.

NUTRITION OBSTACLES: FUELING YOUR BODY WITHOUT THE OVERWHELM

Eating well shouldn't feel like a full-time job. But with all the conflicting advice out there, it's easy to feel overwhelmed or unsure of what really works.

The truth? You don't need a rigid meal plan or a list of "bad foods" to avoid. You just need small, consistent habits that fit your life and make you feel good.

STEP 1: IDENTIFY THE REAL CHALLENGE

Ask yourself: *What's the biggest nutrition habit holding me back? Is it skipping meals, emotional eating, constant cravings, or feeling paralyzed by too many choices?*

Be honest. Name it. Write it down.

STEP 2: UNDERSTAND WHAT'S DRIVING IT

For years, I barely ate during the day. I told myself I was too busy, too focused, too productive to stop and eat. But by the time evening rolled around, I was starving—and anything within reach became dinner. Chips, bread, whatever was quick. Then came the guilt. I thought I had a willpower problem.

But the truth? I was just running on empty.

Once I started eating consistently throughout the day, everything changed. My cravings weren't so intense. My mood evened out. I stopped feeling out of control around food, not because I was more disciplined, but because my body wasn't screaming for fuel anymore.

The problem wasn't the food I was eating at night. It was the pattern I had built during the day.

When you find yourself reaching for food out of nowhere, pause and look a little deeper. Are you truly hungry—or just depleted? Are you craving nourishment, or just trying to fill a gap that opened up hours ago?

Sometimes the real shift isn't about cutting things out. It's about tuning in and giving your body what it actually needs—*before* it gets desperate.

If you tend to skip meals, try setting a reminder to eat just one balanced meal earlier in the day. If you find yourself stuck in cravings, take a moment and ask, Am I actually hungry—or just drained, bored, or stressed? If meal prep feels overwhelming, don't try to fix the whole week. Pick one meal—maybe just breakfast or lunch—and make that a little easier.

You don't need a perfect plan. You just need one simple, doable step that supports your body and fits your life.

Choose it. Try it. And trust that every small step you take in this direction adds up.

Reflection Prompt: What's one small nutrition habit I'd like to shift—and what's one simple step I can take this week to move toward that change?

LOOKING BACK AND MOVING FORWARD

Take a breath and really take in how far you've come. When you first started, maybe you felt stuck, unsure where to begin. Maybe doubt crept in and whispered, *"What if I can't do this?"* Maybe fitness felt like something you could never stay consistent with. Maybe food choices felt more confusing than supportive.

But you didn't give up.
You showed up.

You started noticing the thoughts that held you back and shifted them.
You stopped chasing perfect and started choosing *progress.*
You moved your body in ways that felt doable. Not forced.
You started seeing food not as the enemy, but as fuel that supports your energy and your life.

These aren't small things. They're real, powerful shifts. And they didn't happen by accident. *You created them.*

You're no longer where you started and that matters. You've taken steps toward a life that feels more like *you*. Stronger. More confident. More grounded in what works for your real life.

And now? It's not about starting over or waiting for the "right" time. It's about trusting yourself to keep going. To keep showing up. Not perfectly. But consistently.

Throughout this chapter, we've explored the most common obstacles that show up with nutrition, mindset, and fitness and how small, realistic shifts can create real change.

Now, let's check back in with Emma, Lisa and Jasmine to see how things have unfolded since they started making these shifts in their own lives.

CASE STUDIES

EMMA IN ACTION: TURNING PLANS INTO PROGRESS

Emma didn't overhaul her life. She just started walking. Twenty minutes a day, most days of the week. No music, no fancy gear, just her and the pavement. It became her reset button. Even on days when everything else felt rushed or chaotic, those walks helped her breathe.

The biggest shift? Letting go of the pressure to do it all perfectly. One night, she grabbed a quick frozen meal after a long day and thought, *well, there goes my streak.* But then she paused. Instead of spiraling, she took a moment to notice how she felt and journaled about it. That one choice didn't mean she had failed. It just meant she was human. That mindset shift—that *consistency matters more than perfection*—changed everything.

Emma has also been experimenting with food in a new way. Nothing fancy. She eats one balanced meal a day, something with protein, veggies, and grains. It doesn't always look Instagram-worthy, but it gives her energy. And when the snack cravings hit, she's reaching for things that make her feel good, not guilty: a handful of almonds, a piece of fruit. Nothing complicated. Just better choices, made easier.

Once a week, she rolls out her mat and follows a beginner Pilates video. It still feels unfamiliar, but it's helping her reconnect with her body in a way she hasn't in years. She doesn't push herself to be perfect—just present.

Her journal is becoming a quiet tool of accountability—a space where she tracks what she eats, how she feels, and what's working. She's noticing patterns. With each entry, she's learning more about what her body needs—and that knowledge builds trust.

Emma's not chasing a finish line. She's building a foundation—step by step, choice by choice. And that's the kind of progress that lasts.

LISA IN ACTION: BREAKING THE CYCLE AND MOVING FORWARD

Lisa knows what to do. Her self-assessment confirmed what she already felt—this isn't about starting from scratch. It's about finally sticking with the habits that make her feel strong without burning out.

She's done waiting for the perfect plan and done chasing extremes. This time, she's focused on building momentum that lasts.

The biggest shift? Letting go of the pressure to "get it right." Instead of scrapping her whole routine after a missed workout or takeout dinner, she takes a breath, resets, and moves on. No guilt. No spirals. Just one choice at a time.

Lisa leans into the workouts she loves—cycling twice a week, the wind in her hair, legs pumping, stress melting away. On hectic days, she swaps in a 15-minute Pilates flow or a few rounds of bodyweight moves in her living room—nothing fancy, just movement that fits.

Meal prep, once a dreaded chore, now looks different. Twice a week, she preps a few easy meals and snacks—things she actually enjoys eating. If the week goes sideways, she grabs healthy shortcuts from the grocery store and keeps going. There is no shame, just flexibility.

And maybe most importantly, Lisa's no longer treating a treat like a failure. Most of her meals are balanced and nourishing—protein, greens, healthy fats—but there's also a square of dark chocolate or a glass of wine with dinner. She's fueling her body without the food rules.

What's changed? Lisa's not trying to prove anything. She's not chasing quick fixes. She's creating consistency that feels real and reclaiming trust in herself.

JASMINE IN ACTION: LEVELING UP WITH INTENTION

Jasmine's not just active—she's seasoned. She could easily coast after decades of training, competing, and dialing in her nutrition. But that's not who she is. Jasmine isn't interested in maintaining. She's here to evolve.

Her workouts are powerful, and her meals are purposeful. But now, it's about precision, doing what works even better, with more intention and less wear and tear.

Lately, Jasmine's been shifting her focus from volume to recovery. A younger version of her might have pushed harder. Now, she's getting smarter. Two days a week, she trades in sweat for stretch—mobility flows, long walks, and restorative yoga. Not as flashy, but profoundly effective.

She's also started playing with intensity. Heavier weights. Shorter, focused sessions. New movement challenges like swimming laps or hiking unfamiliar trails. She's keeping her edge—not by doing more, but by doing what matters most.

Her mindset has shifted, too. Jasmine used to see rest as weakness. Now, it's a strategy. She tracks her energy, prioritizes sleep, and listens to her body like a trusted training partner. Recovery isn't a break. It's the bridge to progress.

In the kitchen, Jasmine's already a pro—but even there, she's refining. She's adjusted her protein around workouts, added more anti-inflammatory foods, and cut back on anything that leaves her feeling sluggish. These aren't diet rules. They're performance tools.

And something new is stirring: the pull toward mentorship. Jasmine has begun sharing her story with other women at her local studio, offering encouragement and insight. It's not about becoming a coach but showing others what's possible.

Jasmine's not at the beginning of her journey. She's building her next chapter—with strength, clarity, and a fierce sense of purpose.

YOU'VE FACED THE HARD STUFF—AND YOU'RE STILL MOVING

You've looked at what gets in your way. You've taken small, powerful steps to move through it. That's what real change looks like. Not perfect. Not dramatic. Just honest and steady.

Obstacles will show up again and now you know how to face them with clarity and compassion.

In the next chapter, we'll talk about how to keep going. Because once the spark is lit, momentum is what keeps it alive.

LET'S TURN YOUR PROGRESS INTO SOMETHING THAT STICKS.

CHAPTER 12

KEEPING MOMENTUM

KEEPING MOMENTUM: WHAT HAPPENS AFTER THE FIRST STEPS

You've done the hard work of breaking through obstacles. You've challenged the thoughts that held you back, found ways to move that fit your life, and created a healthier relationship with food. In short, you've proven to yourself that change is possible. Not by doing everything perfectly, but by staying committed even when things felt difficult.

But what happens now?

Momentum is not about quick bursts of motivation. It is about continuing even when the excitement wears off or when progress feels slow. Even when life throws distractions in your path. The real work is not in starting, it is in learning how to keep going.

I learned this firsthand in my journey as a podcaster.

HEIKE YATES

THE MOMENT I WANTED TO QUIT (AND WHY I DIDN'T)

When I first started my podcast, I felt unstoppable. The idea of sharing my voice, connecting with inspiring guests, and bringing real conversations to my audience felt like an adventure. I remember sitting in my home studio before that very first episode. I adjusted the mic. I glanced at my notes. Heart racing, I hit record.

For a moment, doubt crept in: "Is this good enough? Will anyone even listen?" But I kept going. Each episode was proof I was growing. I loved the process. I loved hearing from listeners who said, "That one really hit home." For a while, that was enough.

Then the newness wore off.

The excitement faded, and the behind-the-scenes work started piling up. Booking guests, editing audio, and promoting each episode. It began to feel like another task on a never-ending list. I sat at my desk one evening, staring at my mic, completely drained. *Does this even matter anymore?* That could've been the end. But I made a different choice.

I reminded myself why I started. Not for numbers or praise but because I believed in the power of honest conversations. Because if even one person listens and feels seen or inspired, it's worth it.

So instead of quitting, I adjusted. I gave myself permission to let go of perfection. I simplified. I made the process more joyful. I allowed the podcast to evolve with me.

And something shifted.

Momentum returned, not because I was riding a wave of excitement, but because I was consistent. I showed up, even when it wasn't easy. And that's where the real growth happened, not in the thrill of starting, but in the decision to *keep going.*

NOW, IT'S YOUR TURN

You've come this far for a reason. And when the energy dips or the results don't come as quickly as you hoped, that's not a sign to stop, it's a signal to adjust.

What you've built matters. And what you do next is what creates lasting change.

Let's dive into what it really takes to build momentum that lasts.

You've already done the hard part. You've faced the challenges, adjusted your expectations, and kept showing up, even when it would have been easier to walk away. That's more than progress. That's proof of your strength, your resilience, and your commitment to yourself.

Now it's time to shift your focus, not on what was hard, or what didn't go as planned, but on how to keep moving forward with purpose and clarity. You've laid a strong foundation. This next phase is about building momentum and reconnecting with what makes the journey feel meaningful.

Because real momentum doesn't come from pushing harder or doing more. It comes from staying grounded in your *why*, fueled by what lights you up, and supported by habits that feel like *you*.

And if your spark feels a little dim right now? That's not the end of your story. It's your invitation to pause, reconnect, and rise with even more clarity than before. You haven't lost your way, you're simply being called to return to what matters most.

Mantra:

 I don't have to feel ready. I just have to return to myself. 〞

So let's reignite your spark. Keep it fun, or find a way to make it fun again. That might mean changing your workout playlist, trying something new, joining a class, or simply reminding yourself that this journey is *yours*.

It's not about following rules. It's about creating a rhythm that feels good, energizing, and true to who you are *right now*.

You've already shifted from all-or-nothing thinking. You've learned to listen to your body, fuel it with care, and move in a way that feels supportive, not punishing. That's real progress. That's the foundation of lasting change.

And when those old thoughts try to sneak back in, reminding you of perfection or pressure, pause. Breathe. Come back to your why. Come back to *you*.

You already have the tools. You've done the work. You've been evolving with every step.

Now it's time to trust that.
Trust your process.
Trust yourself.
And keep going, stronger, clearer, and more confident than ever before.

Reflection Prompt:
What's one way I can make this journey feel lighter, more enjoyable, or more me? How will I stay connected to what matters most?

SHIFT YOUR FOCUS TO WHAT'S WORKING

Luna had spent years chasing progress but never giving herself credit for it. Even as she built healthier habits and made better choices, a voice in her head kept whispering, "It's not enough." If her workouts weren't perfect or her meals didn't follow a plan exactly, she'd convince herself she was slipping. The more she focused on what she *should* be doing, the harder it became to see how far she'd already come.

Then one day, mid-thought, something shifted. She caught herself saying, "I should be doing more," but this time, instead of spiraling into guilt, she paused. And she asked a different question: "What am I already doing that's working?"

That small shift changed everything.

Luna started noticing her wins, things she had completely overlooked before. She realized she was already stronger. Already making better choices. Already showing up for herself, day after day. And once she stopped chasing perfection and started recognizing her progress, her motivation returned. She didn't have to force it. She *wanted* to keep going.

If you're feeling stuck right now, it might not be a sign to push harder. Sometimes it's a sign to look closer. Ask yourself: "What's already working?" What habits have you built that you haven't celebrated? What choices are you making, maybe even without realizing it, that support the woman you're becoming?

You already have the tools. You've done the work. This book has guided you through mindset shifts, movement strategies, and the foundations of a healthier relationship with food. If something feels off, you don't have to abandon it all, just return to what's helped you most.

Momentum doesn't come from constantly striving or starting over. It comes from recognizing what's *already* working and using that as fuel to keep going.

Reflection Prompt: *What's one thing I've done recently that I haven't celebrated? How can I use that as motivation to keep moving forward?*

RECONNECT WITH YOUR WHY

Motivation doesn't fade because you're lazy or undisciplined. It fades when you lose sight of *why* you started.

Maybe you began this journey to feel stronger. Maybe you were tired of waking up exhausted. Or maybe you just wanted to feel like *yourself* again, confident, energized, and connected to your body and your life.

But over time, it's easy to slip into a routine. You start checking boxes, following plans, doing all the "right" things. And without realizing it, you drift away from the deeper reason behind it all.

The spark dims, not because you've failed, but because you've stopped remembering what lit it in the first place.

So pause.

Ask yourself:

Why did I start this?
What was I hoping to change—or finally claim?
What kind of life was I imagining when I said, "I'm ready for something different"?

Then look at how far you've come. Are your habits more consistent? Is your mindset lighter? Is movement easier? Do you feel more like *you* again?

These aren't small things. They're your why, in action.

And if you're feeling disconnected from that sense of purpose, go back to the beginning. Revisit the questions you answered. Reflect on the moments when something clicked. Go back to the part of you that believed more was possible.

She's still here.

She hasn't given up.

Because your why isn't just about hitting a goal. It's about how you want to feel, every single day.

It's the vision that pulls you forward when motivation fades. And when you reconnect with that feeling—your true why—momentum returns. Not because you *have* to keep going... but because now, you *want* to.

Reflection Prompt:
What was my "why" when I started? How has it grown or deepened through this journey?

TAKE OWNERSHIP OF WHAT COMES NEXT

Progress isn't always loud or dramatic. Sometimes it's the quiet decision to show up for yourself in a new way. To stop waiting for permission or motivation and to start trusting that you already know what you need.

You've built routines. You've made powerful mindset shifts. You've reconnected with your body in a way that feels real and sustainable. If things feel off right now, it's not a sign to start over. It's a chance to ask, *what's next for me?*

I think of Nina. She had made a lot of changes, moving more, eating with intention, holding boundaries, but she still felt unsure. Not because she hadn't made progress, but because she hadn't yet *owned it.*

One day, she canceled a commitment, not out of avoidance, but because she recognized she needed rest. She told me later, "I used to push through everything. But this time, I chose what I needed, not what I thought I should do."

That moment wasn't flashy. But it was powerful. It was a sign that Nina wasn't just following a plan, she was leading herself.

That's self-trust. That's agency.

It's not about doing more. It's about recognizing how far you've come and choosing to move forward in a way that aligns with the woman you're becoming.

You're not starting over. You're standing on a foundation you built with intention. And the next chapter? You get to write it your way.

KEEP THE MOMENTUM GOING

Momentum isn't just about action, it is also about mindset. You've done the work. You've built habits. You've shown up again and again.

But even with strong routines in place, old thoughts can creep back in. Self-doubt, comparison, and outdated beliefs can pull you off course if you're not paying attention.

That's why this next step matters.

Moving forward isn't just about doing the right things. It's about thinking in a way that supports your growth. It means recognizing what still lingers under the surface and learning how to shift it so it no longer holds you back.

Try this reframe:
Old thought: "If I miss a workout, it means I've failed."
New perspective: Missing one day doesn't erase my progress. It means I am human. What matters most is that I keep coming back.

CONTINUE TO ROOT OUT NEGATIVITY

People often set goals, reach them, and then stop. Others get discouraged when progress doesn't look perfect and start asking, *Why keep trying?* But real progress isn't about getting it right every time. It's about how you grow over time.

Every decade, I've noticed a shift in what matters to me. What I wanted in my 30s looks very different from what I value in my 60s. Life experience has reshaped my priorities and helped me reevaluate what truly feels aligned right now.

That's why it's worth coming back to this work again and again. Revisit this book every few years or whatever rhythm fits your life. Reflect on what you've done, what matters to you now, and what you're ready to let go of. Life changes. Your goals will, too.

Because chasing goals that no longer reflect who you are today doesn't move you forward, it keeps you stuck in someone else's past version of you.

I remember when I transitioned into my home studio. I had moved into a house with a converted garage, and even though I loved the setup, part of me doubted whether it was "enough." Would people expect something more polished, more like the big studios nearby? Would they judge the small space, the walk up the driveway, the lack of high-end finishes?

At first, that mindset clouded everything. I worried it wasn't good enough.

Then one day, a new client walked in and said, "Wow, this is so private. You have everything anyone could possibly need." And just like that, I saw my space through her eyes. It wasn't about the polish, it was about the experience. The feeling. The energy.

This was *my* space. A place where I could teach in my way, create real connection, and hold space for others to thrive, no uniform to wear and no outside expectations.

Once I let go of those limiting beliefs, I was able to fully own what I had built.

So take a moment and ask yourself:
Where in your life are you still holding onto a negative belief that no longer serves you?
What would shift if you started seeing it through a new lens?

CELEBRATING WINS AND PROGRESS

It's easy to focus on what still needs work. On what's not quite perfect. But in doing that, we forget to honor what we've already done. We downplay the effort, brush past the hard choices, and the old belief that still tries to speak up, "I could have done more."

But what if we flipped the script? What if you paused and said, *"I did this. It matters."*

Because celebrating wins isn't about waiting for a massive breakthrough. It's about recognizing the proof that you're showing up. That you're still in it. Still doing the work. Still moving forward.

> *Did you move your body when everything in you wanted to skip it?*
> *Did you pause before reaching for something familiar and choose what you actually needed?*
> *Did you say no when it would have been easier to say yes?*

Those are wins. They're evidence that you're shifting. That you're living with intention—even when it's messy.

So celebrate that.
Claim it.
Because progress isn't just about where you're going, it's about honoring every step it took to get here.

Reflection Prompt:
What are three small wins I've had this week, things I might have brushed past or forgotten to celebrate? What do they say about the progress I've made and the person I'm becoming?

SHOWING UP EVEN WHEN IT FEELS IMPOSSIBLE

The other day, my client Barb walked into the studio after weeks of canceling. She stood in the doorway, hesitating for a second before stepping inside. I immediately smiled and said, "You are here!"

She sighed, dropping her purse into the cubby, "I almost didn't come. I was debating whether I should just wait until next week."

Barb wasn't new to working out. She had started strong, feeling motivated and excited about her progress. But then, life threw curveballs: work stress, unexpected family obligations, and days where she didn't have the energy. One missed workout turned into three. Three turned into two weeks. The longer she stayed away, the harder it became to come back.

She kept telling herself, "I'll start fresh next week" or "I need to be more consistent before this will actually work." She was caught in the cycle of all-or-nothing thinking. She believed that if she couldn't do it perfectly, she shouldn't do it at all. But here she was, standing in the studio after weeks of uncertainty. And that mattered.

I looked at her and said, "But you are here now. You chose yourself today. That is a win."

Her shoulders relaxed, and a small smile spread across her face. "I guess you're right," she said, exhaling. Barb's struggle wasn't about finding time. It was about learning to trust herself again. She had convinced herself that inconsistency meant failure. But every time she showed up, she was proving that she hadn't given up.

RECOGNIZING EVERY KIND OF PROGRESS

Progress isn't just about what you can measure. It's about how you think, how you respond, and how you keep choosing to show up, especially when it would be easier not to.

Did you rest instead of pushing through exhaustion?
That's progress.
Did you catch a negative thought before it dragged you into self-doubt?
That's progress.
Did you return to your routine after a tough week without punishing yourself?
That's *huge* progress.

These moments often go unnoticed. But they are just as important as the workouts completed or the meals prepped. Because they reflect something deeper: the relationship you're building with yourself.

The way you treat yourself *along the way* shapes how the journey feels and how long it lasts.

So don't skip over these wins.

This is what lasting transformation looks like: small, consistent acts of self-respect that carry you forward.

TAKE A MOMENT TO ACKNOWLEDGE YOURSELF

Before you move on, pause. Take a breath.

Think back to where you started, not just the habits or routines, but how you *felt*.

Now look at where you are.

You've made decisions—small, quiet ones—that have added up. You've shifted your mindset, challenged old beliefs, and stayed with yourself through the messy parts.

It's easy to minimize that. To move on to the next thing without acknowledging what it took to get here.

So ask yourself:

> *What have I learned about myself through this process?*
> *What part of me has grown the most?*
> *What would it feel like to fully receive the progress I've made?*

You're not just going through the motions. You're rewriting your story, one choice at a time.
And that deserves more than a passing glance.
That deserves a moment of recognition.

REMIND YOURSELF OF YOUR STRENGTH

You've already made it through some of the hardest chapters of your life. Moments you didn't think you could get through, but you did. You've built strength, not just in your body, but in your mindset, your resilience, and your ability to keep showing up, even when it was hard.

That strength? It's still with you. And it's what will carry you forward.

But let's be honest, women are often told a different story.

That putting yourself first is selfish.

That if you're not constantly sacrificing, you're somehow falling short.

That being a good mom, partner, friend, or daughter means always giving more, even when you're running on empty.

Here's the truth: Taking care of yourself isn't selfish. It's necessary. It's wise. And it's the foundation for everything else.

It's also the example others need to see.

Your kids, your family, your community, they learn by watching how you show up for yourself.

When you prioritize your health, your boundaries, and your energy, you give others permission to do the same.

And if you ever forget what you're capable of, just remember what you've already overcome.

You've done hard things before, and you'll do them again. But this time, you're doing it without abandoning yourself in the process.

Bold Affirmation:
I am allowed to take care of myself. I am allowed to be strong and supported.

ANGIE'S STORY: LEARNING TO CHOOSE HERSELF

Angie is a full-time caregiver to her adult son, who is on the autism spectrum. He lives at home and will always need her support. Her life is unpredictable. Some nights, she gets no sleep because he is up, restless, and unsettled. Other times, he insists on getting a sandwich at midnight or tries to leave unexpectedly.

She is exhausted, constantly on edge, and tied to the house most of the time. If she leaves, there is always the risk that something will go wrong. When Angie first started coming to my studio, she felt guilty for taking an hour away from home. She kept her phone in her hand the entire session, her eyes darting to the screen every few minutes, anxiously waiting for a text or a call. The weight of responsibility never left her. Even while stretching or lifting weights, her mind was somewhere else, always bracing for the next crisis.

Through our conversations, she began to see what kind of support would actually help—and we came up with a plan that felt doable for her. She started asking her husband to step in more. She slowly let go of the belief that she had to do it all alone. At first, she glanced at her phone a little less. Then, one day, she left it in her bag.

Now, about ninety percent of the time, she comes to class without feeling like she has to be on high alert. She moves with more ease, breathes more deeply, and for that one hour, she is fully present in her own body.

Has her situation changed? Not really. But her mindset has. She has learned that caring for herself is not a luxury. It is a necessity.

REFLECTING AND VISIONING: WHAT'S NEXT FOR YOU?

Taking time to reflect is not about looking back with regret or judgment. It is about gathering insight that will help you move forward with confidence. Every experience you have had, every challenge you have overcome, and every shift you have made has brought you here. Now, it is time to ask yourself what's next.

When I first started envisioning my own studio, I saw more than just a space with equipment. I imagined a place where women could show up exactly as they were. No pressure, no comparison, and no rigid expectations. A place where strength was not just about muscles but about confidence, resilience, and the ability to trust yourself again.

At first, my vision was just an idea, something that felt far away. I was still working in other studios, following someone else's structure, and doing things the way they had always been done. But deep down, I knew I wanted something different. The moment I walked into the space that would become my studio, I could see it. Not just the walls or the layout, but the energy of it, the people who would walk through the door, the transformations that would happen there. I did not have every detail figured out, but I knew this was the next step.

That is what visioning is about. It is not about knowing every answer in advance. It is about having a clear vision of what you truly want. It is allowing yourself to take that step, even if you do not know exactly how it will unfold.

I always ask my clients, "In your wildest dreams, what would (fill in the blank) look like?"

Your vision does not have to be grand. What do you want from your life? Do you want more energy? Move without pain? Feel like yourself again? Do you want to be strong enough to lift your suitcase into the overhead bin? Confident enough to take a dance class? Or do you simply want to be at peace with the choices you make for your body?

Whatever it is, own it.

Take agency over your choices, your pace, your progress.

Because when you stop chasing someone else's version of success, you start building a life that actually feels like yours.

Take a moment to see yourself in the future, not just where you want to be but how you want to feel. Picture yourself five years from today. What is different? What have you let go of? What have you built? What is bringing you joy?

Now, bring it back to today.

What is one small thing you can do to take a step toward that vision? It does not have to be a drastic change? From choosing movement that feels good, nourishing your body for energy, or changing the way you talk to yourself, there are many ways to reach your vision. Whatever it is, take that step today.

Your journey does not end here. It is always evolving, always shifting. You have already done so much. Now, it is time to step into what is next.

WILLING TO TAKE RISKS

You have taken time to reflect on where you have been. You have started to shape a vision of where you want to go. But a vision is only as powerful as the actions you take toward it. At some point, you have to stop thinking and start doing. That means stepping into the unknown, trying something new, and being willing to take risks. Because what is the alternative? Staying in the same place, wondering *what if*? Nothing changes if nothing changes.

I have been there too.

When I signed up for my first improv class, I had no idea what I was walking into. Improv—short for improvisational theater—is all about thinking on your feet, speaking without a script, and trusting that you'll figure it out as you go.

I wasn't trying to be an actress, I just wanted to push myself to try something completely out of my comfort zone.

I sat in the waiting area, listening to the chatter of other students who seemed far more comfortable than I felt. The sound of laughter echoed from inside the studio as the class before mine wrapped up. My stomach tightened.

"What if I fail? What if I embarrass myself?"

The thought of stepping onto a stage without a script felt terrifying. But the truth is, the improv gods were not going to come down and tell me, "You are terrible at this. Stop trying."

And even if they did, so what? The worst-case scenario? I wouldn't be great at it. The best-case scenario? I would love it. I took a deep breath, walked through the door, and said yes. Guess what? I *did* love it.

That moment stuck with me because it reminded me of something important. Fear of failure is never as bad as the regret of never trying.

IT'S NEVER TOO LATE TO TRY SOMETHING NEW

My mom is 82 years old, and she has never stopped showing up for life. She spent years working, raising kids, and doing what was expected of her. But she never lost her sense of energy and strength.

Now, she works at a fitness center in a small town near Augsburg, Germany, where people light up the moment they see her. They stop at the front desk just to chat, laughing as she teases the regulars and greets new faces like old friends. She moves with confidence: adjusting equipment, tidying weights, and answering questions without missing a beat.

She is not sitting at home waiting for life to pass by. She is out in the world, engaging, connecting, and proving that age has nothing to do with capability. One day, I called her to check in, and at the end of our conversation, she sighed and said, "You saved me today."

PURSUE YOUR SPARK

She had been feeling restless. Not because she wasn't surrounded by people who valued her, but because she had more to give. More life to live, more stories to tell.

"Mom," I asked, "what is something new you would love to try?"

She laughed, brushing it off. "I don't know, I'm too old to start something now."

I wasn't buying that. I reminded her how strong and capable she still is. How every day she inspires people without even realizing it. I encouraged her to write down her memories: her stories from growing up in Germany during World War II, the lessons she has learned, the experiences that have shaped her. Not just for herself, but for the generations who would love to know her story.

At first, she hesitated. "I wouldn't know where to start."

So, I bought her a book filled with prompts to help her begin. Because why not start now?

We all have moments where we think it's too late, that we've missed our chance. But my mom is proof that as long as you're here, there's still room to grow, to explore, and to try something new.

And maybe that's your invitation too.

Maybe there's something you've been curious about, a class you've wanted to try, a creative outlet calling your name, a form of movement that feels a little intimidating. What if you let yourself explore it, not to be good at it, but just to see what it unlocks?

You don't have to commit forever.
Just once.
Just enough to remind yourself that you're still capable of discovering new parts of yourself.

Because growth doesn't have an age limit.

And trying something new might just reconnect you with a part of you that's been waiting for permission.

Reflection Prompt:
What's one thing I've been curious about but haven't allowed myself to try?
What's one small way I could take that first step?

THIS IS YOUR TIME TO THRIVE

Midlife is not a time to slow down or step aside. It is a time to step forward. To break free from everything that no longer serves you. To claim your strength, your energy, and your confidence for every day ahead. You have already taken the first steps. You have challenged old patterns, shifted the way you think about movement, nutrition, and mindset, and proven to yourself that change is possible.

Before you rush ahead, take a moment. Look back at the path that brought you here.

What shifted in you as you read these pages? What challenges made you stop and think? What ideas stirred something inside you? Growth is not just learning. It is about taking and using what you learned to create something new.

WHAT COMES NEXT

Midlife is not a time to slow down or step aside. It is a time to step forward. To break free from everything that no longer serves you. To claim your strength, your energy, and your confidence for every day ahead.

You've already taken the first steps. You've challenged old patterns, shifted the way you think about movement, nutrition, and mindset, and proven to yourself that change is possible.

But before you rush ahead, pause. Look back at the path that brought you here.

> **"**
> *What shifted in you as you read these pages?*
> *What challenged you?*
> *What stirred something inside you?*
> **"**

Growth isn't just about learning, it's about using what you've learned to live differently. To choose with intention. To move through life as the most aligned version of you.

You don't need a perfect plan. You don't need to have it all figured out. You just need one small action. One next step. One moment of saying, *Yes. I'm ready.*

You've already taken the hardest step: showing up for yourself.

REACHING FOR THE STARS

This isn't the end. It's the beginning of everything you haven't yet imagined.

Midlife isn't about staying in place, it's about rising. Reclaiming. Redefining what's possible and stepping boldly into what you truly want.

You already have the tools. The strength. The clarity. And most importantly, the trust in yourself to use them.

So surround yourself with what lifts you higher. Keep choosing yourself, even when it's hard. Because every day is an invitation to live the life that excites you.

So, what will you do with it?
Whatever it is, don't wait. Step into it. Because the strongest, most powerful version of you isn't ahead of you...

She's already here.

And the best part?

You're just getting started.

ACTION STEPS: KEEPING MOMENTUM

Momentum is not built on one big leap. It is built on the small, consistent steps you take every day. The choices that move you forward, the mindset that keeps you going, and the belief that no matter what, you are capable of growth.

Your journey does not end with this book. It expands from here.

As you move forward, take time to reevaluate your goals. Who you are today is not who you will be five or ten years from now. Your priorities will shift, your desires will evolve, and what once felt important may no longer serve you. That is not a setback. It is growth.

Celebrate your wins. Every single one. The small victories matter just as much as the big milestones. Choosing to move your body when you do not feel like it, making a food choice that fuels you, setting a boundary that protects your energy. Those moments add up.

When doubt creeps in—and it will—challenge it. That voice telling you, *"I am not good enough"* or *"I can't do this"* is not the truth. The truth is, you are learning. You are growing. You are becoming. Replace those doubts with, *"I am capable. I am resilient. I am in control of my own story."*

Keep taking risks. Try something new, even if it scares you. Whether it is a new class, a creative outlet, or a personal challenge, stepping outside your comfort zone is how you keep life exciting. Growth happens when you let yourself be a beginner again.

Set boundaries and prioritize yourself without guilt. Block out time for movement, learning, or rest, and protect it as fiercely as you would any other commitment. You are allowed to take up space in your own life. When things do not go as planned, reflect without judgment.

Ask yourself: "What worked? What didn't? What can I adjust?"

This is not about perfection. It is about learning, adapting, and staying engaged in your own journey. Keep visioning forward. Dream big. Your goals don't have to be practical or perfect. They just have to be yours. What does your happiest, most fulfilled life look like? What is one small step you can take toward it today?

Momentum is not about getting it right every time. It is about showing up for yourself, over and over again. No matter where you are right now, this is just the beginning.

You don't have to have it all figured out. You just have to keep showing up, one intentional choice at a time. This isn't about getting back to who you were. It's about becoming the version of you who's *ready to thrive.*

Let's check in on Emma, Lisa, and Jasmine, each of them taking action, facing challenges, and proving that real momentum is built one step at a time.

CASE STUDIES

This book isn't just about strategies. It's about transformation. It's about breaking free from what's held you back. It's about rediscovering your strength. It's about finally feeling like *you* again.

The journeys of women like Emma, Lisa and Jasmine reflect what so many of us face in midlife, self-doubt, inconsistency, overwhelm. But instead of staying stuck, they used what they learned here to create real, lasting change.

By applying the SPARK Framework, they each found their own way forward. They built momentum, took control of their well-being, and proved to themselves what was truly possible.

Let's see where they are now and how they're keeping that momentum alive.

EMMA'S STORY: FROM OVERWHELMED TO ENERGIZED

> **52 | Busy Professional | Family-Focused | Fitness Beginner**

When Emma first began this journey, she felt stuck. Her energy was low, her clothes fit differently, and her days felt like a blur of responsibilities with no space left for herself. Every attempt at change felt too big, too hard, or too late.

But instead of aiming for an overhaul, she started small: a short walk in the morning, one home-cooked meal a day, and a mindset shift that reminded her that consistency matters more than perfection.

With each small step, something changed.

She started waking up with more energy, noticed how movement helped clear her mind, and, most importantly, stopped waiting for the perfect moment to begin. She was already doing it.

Now, Emma's no longer asking, *"Where do I even start?"* She's showing up for herself daily with more confidence and a stronger sense of control over her health.

And the best part? She finally feels like herself again—clear-headed, steady, and proud of what she's built.

LISA'S STORY: BREAKING THE START-STOP CYCLE

49 | Marketing Consultant | Empty Nester | Fitness Rebooter

In her late 40s, Lisa knew what to do. She'd tried every plan, every challenge, every reset. Her problem wasn't starting—it was staying consistent.

She'd jump into a new routine and feel great for a few weeks...but then life would get busy. Work deadlines, family needs, and the plan would fall apart, and the cycle would begin again.

What changed everything? Realizing that consistency doesn't mean doing everything. It means doing what works for you.

Through this book, Lisa embraced smaller, more realistic shifts. She committed to cycling twice weekly and began weaving in shorter, more flexible workouts. Fitness started to feel fun again, without the pressure to "do it all."

In the kitchen, she simplified her approach. No more complicated meal plans—just balanced, easy meals that actually fit her life.

Now, Lisa doesn't get derailed by a missed workout or a busy week. She adjusts. She keeps going. And for the first time, she's not chasing the next fix. She's living in a rhythm that supports, strengthens, and keeps her grounded.

Lisa's not just staying on track—she's finally in flow. And it shows in how she moves, how she eats, and how she feels.

JASMINE'S STORY: FINE-TUNING FOR PEAK PERFORMANCE

> **61 | Retired Executive | Lifelong Athlete |
> Evolving Her Purpose**

In her early 60s, Jasmine had more than the basics down. She'd run marathons, followed a solid training plan, and fueled her body with intention. She wasn't looking to start over—she was looking to grow further.

This book helped her refine what was already working and challenge herself in new ways.

Instead of pushing harder, Jasmine got more strategic. She added intensity where it counted—heavier lifts and smarter training blocks—and paired it with something she'd often skipped: recovery, stretching, breathwork, and mobility work. These weren't "extras" anymore—they were essential.

She also set micro-goals that kept her motivated without burning her out: a faster mile here, a stronger lift there. These small wins added up.

But the biggest shift? Jasmine stopped defining progress by how hard she worked and started measuring it by how well she recovered, how energized she felt, and how aligned her routine was with her purpose.

She's still a powerhouse, but now she leads with clarity and intention. Jasmine's not just showing up. She's showing up fully—and doing it her way.

TYING IT ALL TOGETHER

You've seen what's possible.

Emma, Lisa, and Jasmine didn't have it all figured out. They didn't wait for the perfect moment or the perfect plan. They just started—one small step at a time.

Each faced doubts, obstacles, and setbacks, but they moved forward anyway—not with perfection, but with intention. And that's what created real change.

Their stories are different, but the message is the same:

You don't need to do it all. You just need to begin.

Start where you are. Stay curious. Keep going.

Because the path to lasting change isn't about doing more—it's about doing what matters most to *you*.

Now, take a moment and turn inward.

Where do you see yourself in their stories?
What mindset shift spoke to you the most?
What's one small action you're ready to take—
not later, but now?

Because this isn't just about their journey.

It's about yours.

You don't need a perfect plan.

You just need a starting point and the courage to take the next step.

CHAPTER 13

TIME TO THRIVE

One evening, my friend Camilla and I decided to check out an Improv show at *D.C. Improv* in Washington, D.C. It was her idea, I had no clue what improv was. I'd been to a stand-up comedy show before, so I figured it would be the same thing. A performer on stage, a microphone in hand, delivering joke after joke to a room full of strangers.

It wasn't.

The theater was packed, buzzing with anticipation. The lights dimmed, and a handful of performers stepped onto the stage, no props, no script, just them and whatever wild ideas the audience threw their way.

Stand-up is a polished act, carefully written, rehearsed, and refined. Improv is the opposite. It's messy, unscripted, unpredictable. One person tosses out an idea, and the rest of the group grabs it, shapes it, and runs with it, no second-guessing, no hesitation. Just trusting the process and going all in.

At first, I watched with curiosity. Then, somewhere between the absurd characters and the chaotic brilliance, something clicked.

PURSUE YOUR SPARK

This is life.

We don't get a script. We don't get a perfectly pre-planned routine that guarantees success. We make it up as we go. And the people who thrive? They're the ones who don't overthink it. They say yes. They step into the unknown. They trust themselves to figure it out along the way.

A few years later, I decided to give Improv a try for myself. Every Sunday at 4 PM, I walk into one of *Imagination Stage's* smaller teaching studios in Bethesda, Maryland, ready for whatever happens next. The room is simple, no stage, just a circle of chairs, bright overhead lights, and an open floor where anything can unfold.

The first few times, I felt completely out of my element. Some of the drills were ridiculous, pretending to mold imaginary substances, building entire scenes from a single word. Sometimes I froze. Sometimes I blurted out something so awkward the whole room burst out laughing, not with me, at me.

But I kept showing up.

And I kept getting better.

That's exactly what this journey is about. Your growth, your strength, your confidence, it's all built in the moments when you choose to show up, take action, and trust yourself. Life is improv. You don't have to be perfect. You just have to step in and play your part.

You've done the work. You've said yes to yourself.
Now it's your turn to step in, trust what you know, and create what's next—one bold, unscripted, beautifully imperfect move at a time.

This is your time to thrive.

LIFE IS IMPROV. YOU DON'T HAVE TO BE PERFECT. YOU JUST HAVE TO STEP IN AND PLAY YOUR PART.

THIS IS YOUR MOMENT

As you step beyond this book, remember:
You don't have to wait for the perfect time.
You don't need every step mapped out.
You just need to begin.

You have the tools.
You have the mindset.
You have the strength.

Now it's about keeping the momentum going.

Keep adjusting. Keep resetting.
Redefine what success looks like, on your terms.

Stop overthinking. Trust yourself.
Take the next step. Then the next.

Trust your body. Stay in motion.
Because *this* is how you thrive.

The only thing left to do is begin.

What's your next move?

HOW TO KEEP THRIVING: THE POWER OF HABITS

Thriving isn't a one-time breakthrough.
It's not about perfection.
It's not about waiting for motivation to strike.

It's about what you do, *again and again.*

That's the power of habits.
The strongest, most energized women don't rely on willpower.
They create simple systems that support them, especially on the hard days.

The secret to lasting change?
Small, consistent actions.

Just like improv, you don't need to know exactly how it will unfold.
You just have to show up, take the next cue, and keep moving forward.

YOUR NEXT STEP: A HABIT CHECK-IN

Before you move on, pause and give yourself credit for how far you've come. Look at your routines with fresh eyes. What habits have already become part of your life, without you having to think about them? Maybe it's how you move your body, the way you prep meals, or the mindset shifts you now catch in real time. These are wins.

Now ask yourself: *What's one small shift you could make today to make those habits feel even easier or more enjoyable?* Maybe it's laying out your clothes the night before, adding music to your movement, or prepping a snack that supports your energy. It doesn't have to be big, it just has to support where you are right now.

And if you're ready to build something new, try stacking it onto something you already do. Pair a mindset moment with brushing your teeth. Add a five-minute stretch after you check your emails. Keep it simple, and make it yours.

Reflection Prompt:
What habit feels second nature to me now and what's one small way I can build on that momentum?

Keep It Simple. Keep It Consistent. Keep Thriving.
You don't have to get it perfect. You just have to keep showing up.

Start small. Let each habit grow from intention, not pressure.
Layer it onto something you already do, make it part of your life, not another thing to check off.

Celebrate every win, no matter how small.
The moments you chose movement, nourished your body, paused to reframe a thought, or said no to protect your energy, those matter. They're the foundation of lasting change.

The more you show up for yourself, the easier it gets.
And the easier it gets, the more progress you make, not because you're striving, but because you're aligned.

This isn't a quick fix. It's a way of life.
A life where you feel strong, steady, and connected to who you are and who you're becoming.

Reflection Prompt:
What's one small habit that's helped me feel more like myself and how can I honor or expand it in this next chapter of my life?

You already have everything you need. Use the Workout Tracker, Meal Prep Guide, Mindset Tips, and additional resources (QR code) to keep the momentum going.

PURSUE YOUR SPARK

YOUR NEXT STEP: BRING SPARK TO LIFE

Before we part ways, take a moment to define what SPARK means to *you* now.

Over the years, I've reimagined it in different ways:

S – Spontaneity
P – Putting in the Work
A – Adventure
R – Reimagining
K – Kick Ass

Now it's your turn.

Make it personal. Make it powerful.
What does SPARK look like in your life?
How will it guide the way you move, think, nourish, and show up moving forward?

Write it down. Say it out loud. Let it remind you who you are and who you're becoming.

A FEW SPARKS FOR THE FIRE

If this book sparked something in you, if you felt seen, heard, or inspired, don't stop here.

The Pursue Your Spark Blueprint is your next step.

It's where we turn insight into action and make your vision of a thriving midlife your new normal. Inside, you'll find structure, support, and a proven process to help you stay consistent and empowered, every step of the way.

More energy. More strength. More *you*. You don't have to figure it all out on your own.

GLOSSARY

ACE Training: A fitness training program developed by the American Council on Exercise, designed to improve strength, flexibility, and overall physical fitness.

Case Studies: Detailed accounts of individuals or groups who have used a specific method (like the SPARK Framework) and their experiences/ outcomes.

Fitness: A state of health and well-being that is achieved through physical activity, good nutrition, and mental wellness practices.

Gap: Refers to the difference between a current state of being and a person's desired state/goal.

Habit-Stacking: Habit stacking is the practice of linking a new habit to an existing one to make it easier to remember and sustain.

Macronutrients: Macronutrients are the three essential nutrients— carbohydrates, proteins, and fats—that provide energy and support overall body function.

Meal Prep: Meal prep is the practice of planning, preparing, and portioning meals in advance to save time, reduce stress, and support healthy eating habits.

Mindset: A mental state and one's approach toward achieving goals, overcoming obstacles, and maintaining motivation.

Nutrition: The process of obtaining the right amount of nutrients necessary for health and well-being.

Obstacles: Challenges or difficulties that may hinder one's progress in reaching their goals.

Pilates: A low-impact exercise system that is composed of controlled movements designed to improve flexibility, strength, and posture.

SPARK: A five-step framework for navigating midlife challenges designed to help you assess your current state, create a realistic plan, take action, overcome obstacles, and maintain momentum toward achieving your goals.

Trap: A behavior or situation that may prevent someone from making progress or achieving their goals.

Visualization: A mental technique where a person imagines themselves in a situation, often used in goal-setting and motivation.

YMCA: The Young Men's Christian Association is known for providing fitness centers and programs that promote healthy living.

Yoga: A physical, mental, and spiritual practice that combines breathing exercises, meditation, and physical poses.

Zumba: A high-energy dance fitness program that combines Latin and international music with choreographed movements for a fun, full-body workout.

ABOUT THE AUTHOR

Heike Yates is a Midlife Fitness Expert with over four decades of experience in fitness, nutrition, and wellness. An American Council on Exercise (ACE) Certified Coach, a Pilates Method Alliance (PMA) Certified Coach, and a Precision Nutrition Certified Sports Nutrition Coach (PN1), Heike's mission is simple: to help midlife women reclaim their strength, energy, and confidence on their terms.

In 2010, Heike founded HEYlifetraining Fitness and Wellness Studio in Silver Spring, Maryland, where she continues to work hands-on with clients, designing personalized programs that are realistic, effective, and sustainable. In 2017, she launched *Pursue Your Spark*, an online platform and podcast that empowers women over 50 through movement, mindset, and lasting lifestyle habits.

In 1985, Heike left Germany to work for the German Foreign Service in Washington, D.C.—a bold leap that brought her a new career, a new culture, and the thrill of independence. But everything changed with motherhood. As a mom of two, she felt the weight of responsibility, the loss of freedom, and the disconnection from the strong, confident woman she once knew. After chasing quick fixes and exhausting routines, she realized what was truly needed: a sustainable, compassionate approach that supported her through every season of life.

That realization became the foundation of her coaching philosophy.

Heike rebuilt her strength from the inside out. She became a competitive bodybuilder, ran ultramarathons, completed an Ironman Triathlon, and created the Pilates with Resist-A-Ball teacher training program, helping people around the world improve strength, balance, and mobility.

Today, Heike is a trusted mentor to women navigating midlife. She proves that this stage of life isn't about slowing down, it's about rising up and redefining what's possible. Whether she's learning how to hold a handstand or teaching herself to play the saxophone without any prior musical training, Heike lives what she teaches: curiosity, challenge, and joy are for every age.

She lives in Silver Spring, Maryland, with her husband Jan. Together, they enjoy triathlons, traveling, Argentine tango, and outdoor adventures. Heike stays closely connected with her two adult children and enjoys regular trips to the Netherlands to visit her grandchildren.

ACKNOWLEDGEMENTS

Writing this book has been one of my most rewarding, challenging and deeply personal journeys. It reflects not just my experiences but also the wisdom, struggles, and triumphs of countless women I've had the privilege of coaching and connecting with over the years. Without them, this book would not exist.

To my husband Jan Amtrup—your unwavering support, encouragement, and belief in me have made every challenge feel lighter and every success even sweeter. Thank you for standing by my side through it all, whether it's calming me with a glass of wine when my website crashes, training for races, dancing tango, or chasing new adventures together. I'm endlessly grateful for your love, your steady presence, and the partnership we've built. You mean everything to me.

To my children, Jesse and Melanie—you have been my motivation and inspiration every step of the way. Watching you carve your paths in life fills me with immense pride. You are the heartbeat of my journey, and my love for you is deeper than words can ever express. Everything I've built, I've built with you in my heart.

To my grandchildren, Lyla and Oliver—your energy, laughter, and curiosity remind me why movement, vitality, and living fully at every stage of life are so important. I cherish every moment we spend together, whether near or far.

To my friends and community—your encouragement, wisdom, and support have been invaluable. Thank you for being my sounding boards, my cheerleaders, and the kind of people who always lift me up.

From the miles shared with my running community to the deep connections built on the dance floor with my tango friends, you've all played a part in my journey. My improv family has pushed me to step outside my comfort zone and embrace the unknown.

To my clients, who are the backbone of this book—your stories, struggles, and triumphs inspired every word on these pages. You are the reason I do this work, and I am forever grateful for your trust, dedication, and willingness to embrace new challenges.

To my publishing team at Reaching and Rooted—Cat Lopez, Katerina Durickovic, and Naomi Moscoe—thank you for your expertise, patience, and belief in this book. Your guidance helped shape this vision into reality, and I am incredibly grateful for your support.

And finally, to every midlife woman who has ever doubted her strength, questioned her worth, or wondered if midlife was the beginning of the end—this book is for you. It's never too late to regain your power, step into your confidence, and create a life you love.

With gratitude,
Heike

APPENDIX A:
PURSUE YOUR SPARK BLUEPRINT

You don't need another health trend.

You need a plan that *works for your life now*—in midlife, with everything that comes with it.

That's exactly why I created the **Pursue Your Spark Blueprint.**

This is an 8-week experience designed to help busy midlife women go from feeling stuck and frustrated to confident, energized, and thriving.

No more all-or-nothing thinking.

No more starting over every Monday.

No more wondering, *"Is this even working?"*

INSIDE THE BLUEPRINT, YOU'LL:

- **Rebuild your energy** with realistic fitness and mindset strategies
- **Create healthy routines** that stick (without overhauling your life)
- **Learn intermittent fasting** in a way that fits your schedule and your body
- **Strengthen your core and body** with targeted Pilates + strength workouts
- **Reclaim your confidence**—in the mirror and in your daily life

It's not just about workouts or meal timing.

It's about consistency, clarity, and confidence.

You'll have full access to all the lessons, resources, and video workouts, plus encouragement straight from me—so you always know what to do and how to keep going.

This isn't a quick fix.

It's a *foundation for your next chapter.*
Because you're not too late.
You're just getting started.
Ready to learn more?
Email me at **heike@heikeyates.com** with **SPARK** in the subject line, and I'll personally send you the details.
Let's build something amazing—together.

APPENDIX B: COACHING ACTION PLAN

YOUR PERSONALIZED FITNESS & NUTRITION BLUEPRINT

Feeling inspired but unsure where to start? You're not alone—and that's exactly why I created these step-by-step protocols. Whether you're new to fitness and nutrition or ready to level up, these **cardio, strength training, Pilates, and nutrition plans** will guide you through a **progressive approach** that fits your lifestyle.

No guesswork, no overwhelm—just **simple, effective steps** to help you build strength, energy, and confidence at any stage. **Let's dive in!**